The Mysterious & Unknown

Alien Abductions

by Stuart A. Kallen

ReferencePoint Press™

San Diego, CA

For more information, contact
ReferencePoint Press, Inc.
PO Box 27779
San Diego, CA 92198
www.ReferencePointPress.com

Picture credits:
AP/Wide World Photos, 88
Dreamstime, 9, 15, 46, 60
Victor Habbick/Science Photo Library, 7, 66, 79, 91
Istockphoto, 21, 25
Francoise Sauze/Science Photo Library, 69
Steve Zmina, 28, 43, 74

Series design and book layout:
Amy Stirnkorb

LIBRARY OF CONGRESS CATALOGING-IN-PUBLICATION DATA

Kallen, Stuart A., 1955-
  Alien abductions / By Stuart A. Kallen.
      p. cm. -- (Mysterious & unknown)
  Includes bibliographical references and index.
  ISBN-13: 978-1-60152-023-4 (hardback)
  ISBN-10: 1-60152-023-9 (hardback)
  1. Alien abduction--Juvenile literature. I. Title.
  BF2050.K35 2008
  001.942--dc22
                                                                2007016584

CONTENTS

FOREWORD

"Strange is our situation here upon earth."
—*Albert Einstein*

Since the beginning of recorded history, people have been perplexed, fascinated, and even terrified by events that defy explanation. While science has demystified many of these events, such as volcanic eruptions and lunar eclipses, some continue to remain outside the scope of the provable. Do UFOs exist? Are people abducted by aliens? Can some people see into the future? These questions and many more continue to puzzle, intrigue, and confound despite the enormous advances of modern science and technology.

It is these questions, phenomena, and oddities that Reference-Point Press's *The Mysterious & Unknown* series is committed to exploring. Each volume examines historical and anecdotal evidence as well as the most recent theories surrounding the topic in debate. Fascinating primary source quotes from scientists, experts, and eyewitnesses, as well as in-depth sidebars further inform the text. Full-color illustrations and photos add to each book's visual appeal. Finally, source notes, a bibliography, and a thorough index provide further reference and research support. Whether for research or the curious reader, *The Mysterious & Unknown* series is certain to satisfy those fascinated by the unexplained.

INTRODUCTION

Visitors from Space

In 2004 Ann Francis said that while living in New York she was kidnapped by gray space aliens, or "Grays," and taken for a ride on their spaceship. Francis, who was 35 years old at the time, later said that the aliens told her to look out the window of the spaceship and remember everything she was seeing. Francis did as instructed and noticed another large spacecraft flying nearby. Inside she could see Grays and humans working together. After a time, Francis was flown to a place that resembled the desert of New Mexico. It was dotted with adobe buildings similar to those constructed by Pueblo Indians. Somehow Francis was transported into one of the buildings, where she saw that the interior was divided into four cubicles. One of the rooms became her new living quarters.

Francis was later escorted around the building by a Gray who pointed out the dining hall and the women's bathroom. Another part of the complex contained a sort of research facility or training camp where the aliens were teaching humans to fly spaceships. Francis said that she sat at a large curved panel outfitted with lights, knobs, and an oval steering wheel that was used as a training module for future UFO (unidentified flying object) operators.

While performing her tasks, Francis said the Grays communicated telepathically with one another and she could hear them thinking that the humans were "training well." [1]

Francis, who described her experience as enlightening and fun, is among thousands who say that space aliens kidnapped them for training purposes. Other abductees have had much more frightening or humiliating experiences, saying they were subjected to painful medical experiments or used for sexual reproduction.

Not Deluded, Lying, or Mentally Ill

According to a 2002 Roper poll conducted for the Sci Fi Channel, 1 percent of Americans, or about 3 million people, say they have had personal encounters with extraterrestrials (ETs). While some doubt the accuracy of this figure, there is little doubt that belief in space aliens and UFOs is widespread. This has helped to create a mini-industry based on alien abductions. In 2007 thousands of people engaged in abduction research or in developing psychological theories on abductees. Others have written about their abduction experiences in countless books, magazines, and articles on Web pages.

Some of the abduction research has been conducted by respected professionals. For example, John Edward Mack, a Pulitzer Prize–winning author, psychologist, and professor at Harvard Medical School, interviewed hundreds of people who claimed to be abductees. They came from all walks of life and include a restaurant owner, secretaries, prison guards, college students, and homemakers. While Mack was struck by the ordinariness of the subjects, after spending hundreds of hours with each one, he came to sincerely believe that they were telling the truth: "The majority of abductees do not appear to be deluded, confabulating, ly-

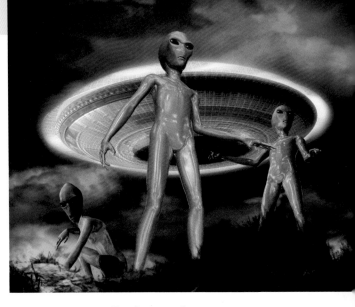

ing, self-dramatizing, or suffering from a clear mental illness."[2] Only one person exhibited psychotic symptoms.

Mack's work generated great controversy. After his 1994 book about the research, *Abduction,* was published, Harvard appointed a committee to investigate his clinical care of patients. While the case was eventually dropped, it was the first time a tenured Harvard professor not suspected of ethical or criminal violations was investigated in this manner.

Human Powerlessness

Mack survived the controversy but, like many abductees, he was subjected to widespread ridicule. Others who come forward with tales of alien abductions are treated as if they are insane. Despite the notoriety attached to such claims, abductees regularly report astounding tales of radiant UFOs filled with bizarre-looking creatures and all manner of inexplicable machinery. The motives of the inhabitants are alternately described as evil, benevolent, or creepy and weird.

Whether the abductees are lying, deluded, hallucinating, or were actually snatched by extraterrestrials remains unknown in most cases. But as science fiction scholar Terry Matheson states, tales of abduction "are intrinsically absorbing; it is hard to imagine a more vivid description of human powerlessness."[3] And as long as people like to hear scary stories about mysterious phenomena, the abductees will capture the attention of ordinary people whose feet remain firmly planted on Earth.

One percent of Americans, or about 3 million people, say they have had personal encounters with extraterrestrials. This picture shows an artist's rendering of aliens landing on Earth.

CHAPTER 1

Kidnapped by Aliens

Every year stories surface in the media about people who claim to have been kidnapped by space aliens. These abductees come from all walks of life and live in nearly every nation on Earth. Some go public with their tales of extraterrestrial kidnapping, appearing on talk shows or writing books. Others share their stories reluctantly, fearful of losing their jobs or becoming targets of scorn. Whatever the case, the abductees share a common bond with one another and are part of what might be called an abduction culture that dates back more than half a century.

The modern era of alien abduction began in the late 1940s when widespread flying saucer mania swept across the United States. In the pre–World War II era, hundreds of UFO sightings were reported over a period of several months. The accounts were picked up by the press and space aliens promptly became

The modern era of alien abduction began in the late 1940s when widespread flying saucer mania swept across the United States. Many photos of flying saucers surfaced but most were proven to be hoaxes.

the subject of sensationalized stories in books, magazines, newspapers, and movies.

By 1947, 90 percent of Americans said that they had heard of flying saucers. Perhaps it is not surprising then that abduction stories began to appear the same year. One concerns an unnamed woman who, while undergoing hypnotic psychotherapy, told Dr. Harold Chibbet that she had been transported to Mars. There she was forced to undergo painful medical procedures at the hands of three giant humanoids, including two women and a bald man. Around the same time, a traveling salesman, Simon

Estes Thompson, revealed to the *Centralia (PA) Daily Chronicle* that he was driving down a rural road when he came upon a spaceship hovering above the ground. Thompson was invited on board by naked, childlike beings who told him they were from Venus. After talking with the aliens about reincarnation and vegetarianism, the earthling left the ship. Although the story appeared in the paper on April Fool's Day, UFO researchers said Thompson seemed to be telling the truth.

Abductee stories continued throughout the 1950s, and they tended to fall into three distinct narratives: the subject narrowly escapes abduction; the narrator sees someone else being abducted; or the subject is abducted and has adventures aboard a spacecraft. Of the latter group, a surprising number reported sexual experiences with the aliens.

Bizarre Brazilian Abduction

While most abduction stories were confined to local news media, the first widely publicized account concerned Antonio Villas Boas, a 23-year-old Brazilian farmer. Boas often worked on the family farm at night to avoid plowing during the heat of the day. On October 15, 1957, around 1 A.M., Boas was working alone in the fields when he saw a reddish light zooming toward him at an astounding speed. Although the light was extremely intense, Boas perceived it to be a spacecraft in the shape of an elongated egg with three legs or landing gear protruding from the underside. As Boas tried to escape, his arm was grabbed by a creature who forcefully pushed him to the ground. The farmer was picked up by three other creatures, lifted off the ground, and dragged to the spaceship.

Boas later recalled with amazing detail the strange appearance of his abductors. He said they wore very tight-fitting suits made of gray, striped material. Their tall helmets were also gray and hid their heads except for their small, blue eyes seen behind goggles. Three silvery metal tubes slightly smaller than garden hoses protruded from the tops of the helmets and disappeared into their clothing. The aliens wore boots with thick, 3-inch (7.5 cm) soles and with curled-up toes like those worn by elves in fairy tales.

In their boots the creatures stood about 5 feet, 4 inches (1.63 m) tall, about the same height as Boas. Yet they were easily able to force him up the ladder through the hatchway of their ship, which closed behind the abductee with no seam or visible opening. Once inside the ship, Boas claims, his captors attempted to communicate with him using unworldly, animalistic sounds. Then, despite his repeated protests the aliens undressed Boas, smeared him with a clear, odorless liquid, and removed a blood sample from his chin, leaving several small scars.

An Astoundingly Beautiful Alien

Boas was placed in a room that contained a gray foam mattress and left alone. After about an hour, a blonde, blue-eyed humanlike woman walked into the room. She was so astoundingly beautiful Boas could only stare at her with his mouth open. Although the woman never spoke, the two made love for about an hour. Before the alien woman left, she smiled at Boas and pointed to her belly, as if to say that she was now pregnant. Eventually, the abductee was given his clothes and escorted off the ship, which promptly took off at an incredible speed, turning multiple shades of bright colors before disappearing into space within a matter of seconds. Upon returning to his tractor, Boas noticed it was 5:30 A.M. About four and a half hours had passed since he was first seized.

During the weeks that followed, Boas suffered from a host of medical problems. Hoping to find a cure he visited a well-respected doctor, Olavo T. Fontès, who was a professor of medicine at the National School of Medicine of Brazil. Fontès discovered that Boas had been exposed to a massive dose of radiation and was experiencing radiation poisoning that resulted in

> pains throughout the body, nausea, headaches, loss of appetite, ceaselessly burning sensations in the eyes, [skin] lesions and the slightest of light bruising . . . which went on appearing for months, looking like small reddish nodules, harder than the skin around them and protuberant, painful when touched, each with a small central orifice yielding a yellowish thin waterish discharge.[4]

After learning of Boas's condition, Fontès convinced the young man to tell his story to a Brazilian military intelligence agent. The army officer interviewed Boas and gave him a series of physical and psychological tests, finally concluding that Boas was telling the truth about his abduction. In the years that followed, Boas became an attorney in the city of Formosa. He stuck by his story for 35 years until his death in 1992.

Betty and Barney Hill's Close Encounter

Several years after the Boas story circulated, another even more fantastic abduction story came to light in the United States. And the ET kidnapping of Betty and Barney Hill remains among the most popular and detailed alien abduction stories in history.

The story began on September 19, 1961, when the Hills, a married couple from Portsmouth, New Hampshire, were driving home from a vacation at Niagara Falls in Canada. While traveling through the dense forests of the White Mountains on U.S. Route 3 the Hills saw a bright starlike light in the sky that appeared to be following them. As they passed an isolated spot called Indian Head, Barney had the sudden urge to stop the car, walk into the dense woods, and study the star through his binoculars. Betty stayed by the car, tending to the couple's dog.

Barney was staring through his binoculars as the object, described as a giant flying pancake or banana with a long row of windows, abruptly came within 100 feet (30.5 m) of him. Later, Barney said that it was obviously a UFO, and inside he spotted space aliens dressed in Nazi-like uniforms. Barney panicked, jumped into the car with Betty, and the couple drove off.

UFO Confirmed by Radar

During the ride home the Hills experienced a strange sort of time warp that has become commonplace in alien abduction experiences. First they heard a beeping, which Betty compared many years later to the sound made by a microwave oven, which had not been invented in 1961. Next, time seemed to stop. The Hills then heard another beeping followed by a bump. The couple looked around and realized that they were inexplicably 35 miles (56.3 km) away from where they had seen the UFO. They had no recollection of what happened between the beeping sounds. When they finally reached Portsmouth, the Hills realized that it had taken them seven hours to drive a mere 190 miles (305.8 km), a distance usually covered in about four hours.

The next day, after the Hills returned home, they began to notice odd occurrences. Barney's shoes were scuffed as if they had been dragged along the ground, and he was experiencing extreme back pain. Distressed, the couple decided to report their experiences to officials at a local air force base. There, Major Paul W. Henderson allegedly told Betty, "The UFO was also confirmed by our radar."[5]

Betty's Dreams

At first the Hills did not believe that they had been abducted. However, Betty began having disturbing, recurrent nightmares in which she was forced to walk through a forest by two alien men who were about 5 feet (1.5 m) tall and bald with large bulbous foreheads. The aliens wore matching uniforms and caps that were similar to those worn by air force personnel.

In Betty's dreams Barney was alongside her but appeared to be in a trance. The dreams continued with the Hills and the aliens walking up a ramp into a metallic, disc-shaped vessel. Then Betty was taken to a separate room and commanded by an English-speaking alien to cooperate with a man called the "examiner." This creature had a pleasant demeanor and Betty remained calm as he inspected her hair, eyes, mouth, hands, and feet. The exam took a frightening turn when the alien informed Betty he was going to conduct a pregnancy test. He removed her dress and plunged a 6-inch (15.2 cm) needle into her navel, causing Betty to scream in agonizing pain. However, the examiner waved his hand over her wounded stomach and the pain vanished. Betty was soon reunited with Barney.

When it appeared the abduction was about to come to an end, Betty says she asked the alien for a memento of her visit to prove

Many who claim to have been abducted describe the alien vessel to be metallic, disc-shaped, and glowing with lights.

that she had been aboard a UFO. The alien gave her a book filled with symbols listed in columns. Betty then asked an alien where he was from and the creature pulled down a map filled with stars, planets, and marks indicating trade and expedition routes. The alien asked Betty to find Earth on the map, but when she could not do so he told her that she was too ignorant to understand what part of the universe he was from. Finally, the couple left the spaceship, but not before an alien confiscated the book he had given Betty, explaining that he did not want the Hills to remember anything after they left.

Dreams or Reality?

Continually haunted by her dreams Betty decided to undergo regressive hypnosis, a type of therapy meant to unlock hidden

Betty's Star Map

When Betty Hill was under hypnosis recalling her abduction, her doctor, Benjamin Simon, asked her to draw the "star map" she had purportedly been shown by the aliens. Although she was unsure that she could reproduce the intricate, three-dimensional map she had been shown, with Simon's coaxing she eventually drew a map that contained twelve stars. In 1969, more than five years after she underwent hypnosis, Betty was interviewed by amateur astronomer Marjorie Fish, who determined that the map matched a star system called Zeta Reticuli, located 39 light years from Earth. Zeta Reticuli is barely visible to the unaided eye and can be seen only from tropical locations south of Mexico City.

Fish later claimed that Zeta Reticuli was home to a race of aliens called Grays or Zetas. Since that time ufologists have come to believe that Zetas travel to Earth to study human life and genetic engineering. They are said to have played a part in the alteration of genetics over the centuries and are trying to crossbreed with humans in order to create a superior "mixture race."

memories in the subconscious. In December 1964, with some trepidation, the Hills visited an expert in the field, Boston doctor Benjamin Simon, who conducted a series of hypnosis sessions, first on Barney, then on Betty.

Barney's therapy became extremely dramatic when he became emotional, angry, fearful, and hysterical under hypnosis. While suffering through obvious mental and physical pain, Barney recalled meeting six aliens in the woods. However, he was so fearful that he kept his eyes tightly shut during most of the encounter. Somehow Barney was still able to see, and he remembered being taken to a room, as in Betty's dream, and examined by creatures who scraped his skin and peered into his eyes and mouth. The aliens also inserted a probe in Barney's anus and placed a cuplike device over his genitals.

Betty's hypnosis was less dramatic and her description of the event differed little from her dreams. After analyzing the accounts for some time, Simon reached a somewhat ambiguous conclusion. While deciding that the Hills truly believed they had been abducted, the experience was a fantasy. However, the imaginary experience was a reaction to seeing a real UFO, although the Hills were never abducted and brought on board the spacecraft.

As Seen on TV?

Simon's analysis has been dismissed by skeptics who say Betty's dreams were flights of fancy caused by her fascination with UFOs. They point out that in the weeks before the encounter Betty read a book about aliens by Donald Keyhoe called *Flying Saucers Are Real*. In addition, 12 days before the hypnosis sessions Betty and Barney allegedly saw the "Bellero Shield," an episode of the TV science fiction program *Outer Limits*. This show featured a space alien similar to the one that appeared in Betty's dreams.

Whatever the cause of the Hills' distress, the hypnosis seemed to help. Betty no longer had nightmares about the incident, and Barney's stress-related illnesses went away. The Hills went back to their daily lives, speaking occasionally to friends and researchers about their purported alien abduction. However, several months after the hypnosis sessions concluded, in October 1965, the *Boston Traveler* printed a front-page story, "UFO Chiller: Did THEY Seize Couple?" Apparently reporter John H. Lutrell had obtained Simon's notes about the incident and also found interviews the Hills had granted ufologists. The day after the Hills' story was printed in the *Traveler,* it was picked up by United Press International (UPI) and published in newspapers across the globe. Overnight, the Hills were famous, with reporters, television writers, and journalists clamoring to hear their story. Writer John G. Fuller gained the couple's trust, and in 1966 he published his book *The Interrupted Journey* about their case. The book also contained a picture of the star map Betty was supposedly shown by the alien.

Barney passed away from a cerebral hemorrhage in 1969 at the age of 46 but the story of the Hills' abduction refused to die. Meanwhile Betty became known as the Grandmother of All Abductees and continued to give interviews until her death in 2004 at the age of 85.

Media-Star Abductees

Whatever the reality of Betty and Barney's story, their case became a media sensation after it was depicted in a 1975 documentary-style television movie *The UFO Incident.* Seen by millions, the movie caused the number of abduction claims to skyrocket. For example, there was a total of 50 abduction reports between 1947 and 1975. However, in the 24 months after the broadcast, there were about 50 a year, a 2,500 percent increase. And, unlike the Hills, who never made money from their experience, the new breed of abductees seemed to be out to achieve celebrity status. For example, 2 weeks after *The UFO Incident* was shown, Travis Walton, a worker in an Arizona logging camp, disappeared for 5 days. After he reappeared, he claimed to have been abducted by aliens.

Combining elements of the Hill and Boas abductions, Walton said he met up with gray aliens that appeared alongside beautiful blond aliens. Walton's case was an immediate sensation and he was quickly signed to write a book, *The Walton Experience,* which was published in 1978. It was made into a movie in 1993. Today, Walton has his own Web site and makes appearances at UFO conventions and on cable TV shows.

By the 1980s the abduction industry had become big business, with a public eager to hear ever-more-bizarre tales of space kidnappings. Perhaps the apex of this phenomenon came in 1987 when Whitley Strieber, a well-known writer of horror novels, published *Communion,* the first alien abduction story to become a *New York Times* best seller. *Communion* is a purportedly autobiographical account about alien "visitors" who came to Strieber's cabin in upstate New York. Filled with frighteningly bizarre stories and explicit alien sex, *Communion* has been widely criticized by those who say the author simply combined accounts from other abductees into a story that he claims as his own. And when questioned about the book's authenticity, Strieber freely admits that before writing it he read thousands of UFO reports and watched dozens of movies about alien abductions. Skeptics of the abduction phenomenon point out this is typical in many abduction cases, has served to obscure the division between truth and fiction, and causes new abductees to repeat details from old cases. As Harvard psychology professor Susan A. Clancy observes:

> Abduction reports were being published at an ever-increasing rate. They seemed to feed on one another. Each new account absorbed details from previous accounts. . . . Betty and Barney Hill got their ideas from books, movies, and TV. From then on, people got their ideas from books, movies, TV, and Betty and Barney Hill—and whoever the next media-star abductee happened to be.[6]

Painful Medical Procedures

Even with this "echo effect" caused by the media, the alien abduction phenomenon began to change by the late 1980s. Previously, abductions were described as one-time events in which victims would be kidnapped by aliens, examined, and returned to Earth never to see their captors again. However, an increasing number of people started to claim that they were snatched on several occasions, as were members of their families. For example, an abductee named Angie (many abductees reveal only their first names in order to protect their identities) told researcher Budd Hopkins that she had first been abducted as a child in the 1980s and was kidnapped at least three more times in subsequent years. Angie, who is seen as extremely trustworthy because she is in the military and has a high-security clearance, said her mother and possibly her sister have also been abducted.

Angie claimed that she was subjected to painful medical pro-

Many believe that aliens are getting ready to reveal themselves to everyone on Earth. This is based on testimony from recent abductees claiming they have been trained to fly small spacecraft, making them hover in one place.

cedures that included what she called a coring device to extract cellular material from her leg. This is another recent phenomenon, since most early medical procedures described by abductees were passive and noninvasive. These examinations often involved some kind of X-ray or MRI (magnetic resonance imaging) machine that one person described as a big eye that passed over his body. Even when Betty Hill claimed that a large needle was pushed into her navel, she described the experience as painful but quick. In recent years, however, grotesque medical procedures had become a common aspect of abductions, as Mack writes in *Abduction:* "Instruments are used to penetrate virtually every part of the abductees' bodies, including the nose, sinuses, eyes, ears, and other parts of the head, arms, legs, feet, abdomen, genitalia, and more rarely, the chest. Extensive surgical-like procedures done inside the head have been described, which abductees feel may alter their nervous systems."[7]

Such is the case of Paul from New Hampshire who says his abductions began when he was only 6 in 1976. During an experience in the late 1990s, Paul was visited by a glowing light force that made him lie on an examining table while it opened up a 7-inch-long (17.8 cm) cut in his right thigh using some sort of laserlike light tool. Although there was no blood or pain, Paul could see the muscles, ligaments, and veins inside his leg, which caused him to feel terrified and confused. The alien removed a small piece of thigh bone and closed up the incision using the same light tool.

Ready for a Mission to Earth

While abduction tales seem to be growing more and more morbid, another developing trend is the belief that the aliens are getting ready to reveal themselves to everyone on Earth. This hypothesis is based on several recent abduction reports about aliens training older abductees to perform certain tasks. For example, a 51-year-old woman known as Jenny described being taken aboard a UFO and trained to drive a small spacecraft, making it hover in one place. The exercise was a practice rescue mission and Jenny was told to imagine a situation where an alien was on the ground below pursued by a group of angry people. Like a helicopter pilot rescuing a flood victim on a rooftop, Jenny purportedly learned how to steady the UFO, lower a ladder, and save the distressed alien from danger. After she successfully accomplished this procedure, she was given new tasks to learn.

David M. Jacobs, a college professor who founded the International Center for Abduction Research, has heard of a dozen similar cases in which abductees in their 50s were trained to do specific tasks. It is his belief that the aliens would not be training older abductees if they were not planning to use them in the near future, before they become too old to perform the activities skillfully. As Jacobs writes: "It seems unlikely that they were planning to use them forty years from now when they are in their nineties. More likely they are planning to use them while they are alive and vigorous. If that is the case, then they would probably have to fulfill their functions within the next twenty years or so."[8]

For those who believe that aliens are superior beings with a nearly limitless knowledge of this world, it is entirely plausible that they are training humans for a mission to Earth. Whatever the case, alien abduction stories continue to surface. While they receive much less publicity than they did in the 1960s and 1970s, stories of kidnappings by extraterrestrials have become a permanent fixture of modern culture. And as long as human beings gaze into the great mystery of outer space and wonder who or what is out there, it is doubtful that the fascination with alien abductions will end any time soon.

CHAPTER 2

Alien Life Forms

I n September 1880, vacationers at Coney Island, New York, witnessed a flying man maneuvering in the sky overhead. This man had huge bat wings and, according to the *New York Times,* "wore a cruel and determined expression."[9] The creature, described as a mothman, took off toward New Jersey and disappeared forever. During the decades that followed others would describe seeing batlike aliens along with those that resembled devilish monsters, praying mantises, or prehistoric flying pterodactyls. However, since the beginning of the UFO craze in the 1950s, most of those experiencing human-alien encounters report seeing three main types of space aliens: Nordics; Reptilians or Reptoids; and Grays, sometimes referred to as Zetans or Reticulans because they are said to originate in the Zeta Reticuli star system.

A Galaxy of Grays

Grays are by far the most commonly seen alien type, described in 75 percent of abduction cases. Abductees say Grays are around 4 feet (1.2 m) tall, weigh 60 to 90 pounds (27 to 41 kg), and have scaly gray skin, sometimes with a bluish or greenish tint. The creatures seem to have no skeletal or muscular structure, and the body is completely hairless with no visible genitals. They have short legs with elongated arms that allow their three- or four-fingered hands to reach well below the knee. Their bulbous heads are large, but their noses and mouths are very small. They have no lips and no visible teeth. The eyes of the aliens are often described in great detail by abductees who say they are wraparound or slanted toward the back of the skull, very large and black as if covered with lenses.

Grays, as shown here, are by far the most commonly seen alien type. Abductees say Grays are around four feet tall, weigh 60 to 90 pounds, and have large heads, big shiny black eyes, and scaly, gray skin.

Gray aliens have long been part of popular culture. Science fiction author H.G. Wells first described them in his 1901 book *The First Men in the Moon.* In 1947 Grays were alleged to have been victims of a spaceship crash near Roswell, New Mexico, where their bodies were viewed by both military and citizen observers. In the decades that followed, the so-called Roswell aliens were described countless times in the media. Because of the widespread popularity of the Roswell incident, Grays were the type of aliens seen in the blockbuster movies *E.T.—The Extra-Terrestrial* and *Close Encounters of the Third Kind.* In more recent years Gray-type aliens starred in the TV shows *Babylon 5* and *Stargate* and in the cartoons *South Park* and *American Dad.* Grays have even been featured in video games such as PlayStation2 *Destroy All Humans!*

Skeptics believe that abductees are simply describing aliens that are ubiquitous in the media. Ufologists say that Grays are commonly seen because they visit Earth in large numbers and are actively involved in abducting human beings. These extraterrestrials are often said to be benevolent visitors who simply want to help humans evolve. As the author known as Dragonbane explains on the *Above Top Secret* Web site, "They are here to guide humanity into the next millennium with spiritual understanding of each other, in order to create a more perfect society." [10]

Gray Conspiracy Theories

But there is also a darker view of the Gray invasion; some believe the aliens are working with agents of the U.S. government to take over the world and dominate the human race. Conspiracy theorists say that evil Grays were involved with Nazis during

World War II, took part in the assassination of President John F. Kennedy in 1963, and even helped coordinate the terrorist attacks of September 11, 2001.

Even those who doubt such notions seem to agree that Grays are interested in Earthlings only because they want to harvest human sperm, ova, and other genetic material. This theory is based on the belief that, because they all look alike, Grays are clones and therefore have intimate knowledge of creating life through artificial means. The problem, say believers, is that the cloned Grays are becoming inbred after creating many generations from a singe genetic sequence. To solve this problem, the Grays are working to perfect an alien-human hybrid. Some abductees have allegedly witnessed the results of such experiments, describing alien-human hybrids kept alive in fish tanks. Nonetheless, the Grays have had some unexplained problems in trying to perfect the hybrid process and must continue to abduct humans as subjects for their breeding experiments.

There is a sinister offshoot of the clone theory that posits that the U.S. government is working with the aliens. Believers say that the Central Intelligence Agency (CIA) has built huge underground laboratories, known as Groom Lake, Area 51, or Dreamland, in the isolated Nevada desert. In this top-secret facility, 90 miles (145 km) northwest of Las Vegas, the Grays have conducted horrific biomedical experiments on human guinea pigs since the 1950s. The government has aided in the process, exchanging military protection for alien spaceship technology. The thinking goes that after the Grays create a flawless alien-human clone, they will work with the government to create a New World Order where most human beings will be used as slaves.

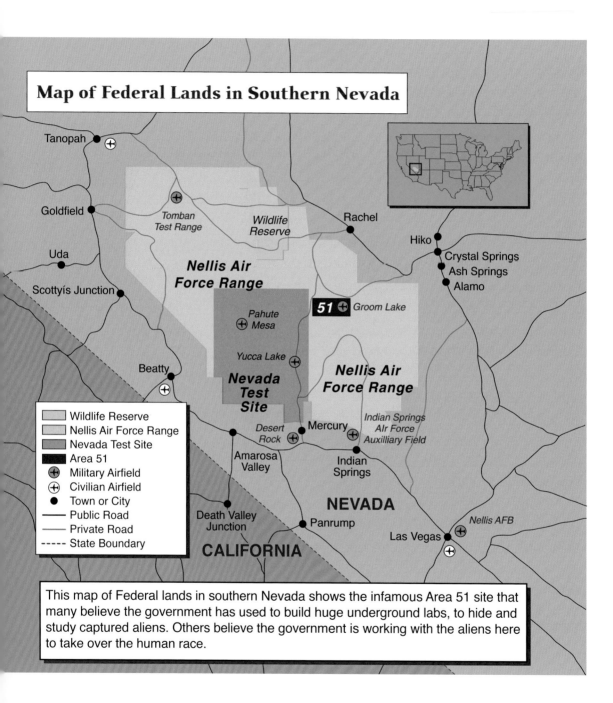

Map of Federal Lands in Southern Nevada

Tanopah

Goldfield

Tomban
Test Range

Wildlife
Reserve

Rachel

Hiko

Crystal Springs

Ash Springs

Uda

Scottyís Junction

**Nellis Air
Force Range**

Alamo

51 ⊕ Groom Lake

Pahute
Mesa

Beatty

Yucca Lake

**Nevada
Test
Site**

**Nellis Air
Force Range**

Indian Springs
Air Force
Auxilliary Field

Desert
Rock

Mercury

Amarosa
Valley

Indian
Springs

NEVADA

Nellis AFB

Death Valley
Junction

Panrump

Las Vegas

CALIFORNIA

Wildlife Reserve
Nellis Air Force Range
Nevada Test Site
Area 51
⊕ Military Airfield
⊕ Civilian Airfield
● Town or City
— Public Road
— Private Road
----- State Boundary

This map of Federal lands in southern Nevada shows the infamous Area 51 site that many believe the government has used to build huge underground labs, to hide and study captured aliens. Others believe the government is working with the aliens here to take over the human race.

The Horrendous Reptoids

There are those who believe that Grays themselves are physically controlled by a superior lizardlike alien race known as Reptilians or Reptoids. The Grays act as the brains or intellect for the Reptoids and are able to work in consort with the U.S. government to provide the aliens with human blood and other bodily fluids that they need to survive. The Reptoids rub these fluids, which may also come from animals such as goats or cows, on their skin to absorb the liquid protein into their bodies.

According to abductees who have interacted with Reptoids, the creatures are 5½ to 9 feet (1.7 to 2.7 m) tall, possess bright red eyes, and look like lizards. They have scales on their backs and greenish brown, scaly skin. Their mouths contain different-sized teeth, including fangs. Reptoids, which have lean bodies, walk upright on muscular legs and have long arms with three elongated fingers and an opposable thumb. Their feet resemble those of Earth lizards with one toe pointing backward, but they have only three clawed toes on each foot. Abductees have seen Reptoids with and without tails.

Unlike Grays, whom abductees describe as either friendly or emotionless, Reptoids inspire nearly universal terror. Oftentimes female abductees claim they were raped by Reptoids, and both men and women say the aliens somehow suck the life out of them. An example is provided by an anonymous abductee working with Aileen Garoutte, a hypnotist who specializes in UFO cases:

> The attacks are horrendous. During each attack I am . . . assaulted in many perverse and sadistic ways. My attackers also feed on me. By feed, I mean they actually consume my life force (spiritual energy).

They are life force vampires (spiritual vampires). I cannot overly stress the importance of that. They also take biological fluid from me that they later consume. They use an advanced form of mind control technology on me in an attempt to turn me into some evil, sick, and depraved individual. They also have tried to make me commit suicide. Once, I was under the control of their mind control devices. It felt as if my mind was not my own. . . . I am in constant pain. Most of the time I feel extremely lethargic. I experience constant severe headaches accompanied with occasional nosebleeds. I have pain around my spleen, liver, kidneys, and heart area. The heart area is the area that the demons feed on the most.[11]

According to the victim, the Reptoids have been coming to Earth for thousands of years. They have perfected means for assuming human forms and have infiltrated all aspects of society, obtaining powerful positions in government and industry.

With their superior mental powers, the Reptoids can also enter the minds of their victims and cause them to hallucinate and live in a dream world that is disconnected from reality. This allows Reptoids to manipulate and control the abductees through the use of bizarre illusions called Astral Dreamscape Manipulation. Reptoid researcher James Bartley describes this mind-control technique:

Astral Dreamscape Manipulation is a very pervasive form of behavior modification that most abductees experience at one time or another. Sadly, most abductees are oblivious to the fact that this is an aspect of behavior modification that is routinely practiced by the reptilians upon certain categories of abductees.

. . . There is also a "filthiness factor" associated with [Astral Dreamscape Manipulation]. . . . The atmosphere seems to be saturated with their foul energy. What appears to be feces may be scattered on the floors. Bathroom or locker room scenes are typified by their filthiness. Large cockroaches and other bugs may be seen scurrying around in the astral dreamscape. Large rats are often seen in a dreamscape polluted by the reptilians. These are just a few of the things that are described again and again in the astral dreamscape which create an atmosphere of foul malevolence whenever the reptilians are attempting to manipulate the human's perceptions and emotions. It is altogether apt if you ask me. Vermin such as huge cockroaches and rodents are symbolic of the putrid essence of the reptilians, sewer scum that they are.[12]

The Draco Reptilians

If the evil Reptoids are not frightening enough, they too have their masters, the 12-foot-tall (3.7 m) Draco reptilians that are considered the nobility of the Reptoid hierarchy. While there are fewer reports from abductees about these lizard kings and queens, those who have seen the Dracos say that the aliens are different from regular Reptoids in that they have wings. These consist of long, thin bones or ribs covered with flaps of leathery, brownish black skin attached at the back. Dracos also have horns that protrude from above their brows. These conical horns are blunt and might be used to "hear" vibrations or communicate telepathically.

While the Dracos rule the common Reptoids, they too are ruled by a superior group known as the Draco Prime. An anonymous poster on the Karinya Spiritual Awareness Web site describes the Draco Primes and their plans for world domination:

> It is the intent of the [Draco Prime] Reptoids to create a new race and control it as well as the rest of humanity. There is information available that there are Humans, controlled completely by [Reptoids] living below the surface of the Earth, who have never seen the surface. [Draco Primes] are also engineering new bodies for themselves to occupy . . . because theirs no longer satisfy them. They resort to cloning and stealing of Human embryos to study to determine which is the best soul receptacle for themselves. It is their plan to switch physical realities [with humans]. The Reptoids have created "vats" which are a grouping of ingredients they will use for the new race. Missing persons often go there, especially missing children. . . . Each year they take 10 percent more children whose bodies are stress tested to determine DNA modification requirements. The Draco Primes "feed" only on negative energy. . . . [These] alien beings abduct Humans and subject them to cruel and torturous deaths . . . in order to create a "maximum energy

transfer." Extreme fear and anxiety . . . fuels these beings and keeps them going as one of their forms of nourishment.[13]

Reptilian-Gray Crossbreeds

While Dracos allegedly survive on human body fluids, another type of alien, a type of Reptilian-Gray crossbreed, is said to drink the blood of farm animals. These creatures are sometimes referred to by their Spanish name, Chupacabra (Goat-Sucker), since they were first seen in 1987 abducting and killing goats in Puerto Rico. Since that time they have also been seen in Mexico, Colombia, Argentina, Brazil, the Dominican Republic, Russia, and in the United States in Florida and the Pacific Northwest. Those who claimed to have seen the nocturnal Chupacabra report that they are about 5 feet (1.5 m) tall, have red, slanted eyes, gray fur or skin, no ears, a tiny mouth with no lips but sharp, protruding fangs. There are shaped like Grays but their bodies are like that of a dinosaur that walks upright on its back legs. Some are said to have wings or leatherlike skin on their backs, resembling a cape. The eyes of these aliens are said to have a hypnotic quality that mesmerizes their prey and allows them to puncture the animal's belly and suck its blood and organs through the hole. The aliens are also able to sneak up on their prey because their hair color changes, chameleon-like, to blend in with surrounding vegetation. According to witnesses, they are also extremely fast and can leap 20 feet (6.1 m) in a single bound, even jumping over trees.

Because of the aliens' appearance, ufologists hypothesize that Chupacabra are the results of a breeding experiment that mixed Gray alien DNA with that of the Reptoids. However, some claim that the Chupacabra are rabid coyotes or a human breeding experiment gone awry. This theory postulates that true Reptilian-Gray crossbreeds have black eyes with vertical slits for pupils, short stubby feet, and no toes.

Noble Nordics

Not all aliens are blood-sucking, evil entities with a propensity to kidnap humans and perform unspeakable experiments on them. According to ufologists, extraterrestrials known as Nordics visit Earth in order to watch over humans and guide them through difficult times. And the Nordics, so called because they resemble Scandinavians, are so tall, platinum blond, and handsome that they are sometimes mistaken for angels.

Nordics purportedly come from the star system Pleiades, also known as the Seven Sisters, approximately 440 light years from Earth. Because they live on the planet Telosia in the Pleiades system, Nordics are also referred to as Pleiadeans and Telosians. Because Telosia is allegedly hot and dry with lower levels of oxygen in the atmosphere, the Nordics possess larger lungs than earthlings and have copper instead of iron in their blood to carry oxygen more efficiently. Nordics have two sets of eyelids, and the inner lid allows them to see ultraviolet light invisible to the human eye. Although their brains are similar to humans, they have an extra lobe in the midbrain that allows them to communicate telepathically. This brain also gives Nordics telekinetic powers; that is, they can move objects, even people, with their minds. For example, a Louisiana abductee named Meehan was moved by Nordic aliens through the walls of underground structures, down hallways, and through tunnels. During her abduction she saw human beings preserved in large tubes full of water tended to by earthlings and short aliens. She was later transported to a fantastic garden where a Nordic with long blond hair and loose white robes silently observed her.

According to ufologists, most Nordics do not remain silent but rather try to help humans by giving them important messages. The theory is that the Nordics landed in 1953 at Homestead Air Force Base near Miami, Florida. They allegedly abducted several air force officers in order to warn them about the evil deeds Grays and Reptoids had in store for the human race. Since that time Nordics have also purportedly provided warnings to people about cataclysmic events and future world wars. However, the forewarnings are given in polite and respectful tones and the Nordics answer questions and provide reassurance that is described more as enlightening than depressing. For example, Donna, a Kansas housewife, was abducted several times by a Nordic she calls Peter, who wore a sparkling white uniform. He somehow transported her instantly from her bed to the interior of his UFO. According to abduction researcher Donald Worley:

> Once they were in the UFO her nightgown was removed and she was instructed to stand under a red light that caused her to feel electrified. . . . [A] device that Peter called a "Monotron" was implanted at the base of her brain. . . . [Afterward Donna] received Earth devastation messages as well as many other predictions. . . . In the next abduction she was taken to a huge awesome throne room in a huge craft. . . . She was given another light treatment, drank a hauntingly beautiful blue liquid, and received an implant through her ear. Later Donna was privileged to see many things and learn much.[14]

Most of Donna's predictions are similar to those found in the Bible, particularly the Book of Revelation, which predicts an apocalypse and the end of life on Earth. Nonetheless, Donna considers her experience with the Nordics positive, saying that she can now "look at the Bible with the understanding of advanced intelligence."[15]

This theme was reiterated by Sarah, a 58-year-old woman who lives in the rural woods of northern Minnesota. Sarah says she was abducted 11 times, beginning at the age of five. During a 1990 experience, Sarah was abducted by a UFO in her front yard but experienced no fear when she was told by Nordics that the end of time was near, and all life on Earth would cease by 2011. Worley writes that the Nordics might be passing on such messages because they "are engaged in a great abduction project intent on salvaging some of the inhabitants [of Earth, or are] . . . simply intent on elevating humanity to a higher plane of existence . . . watching to see if our emerging planetary civilization, which is still aboriginal, warlike and dangerous, does not so pollute or poison its own planet that it fails to survive."[16]

A Long History?

The tales of Nordic aliens are only the most recent in a long line of "white" spirits or gods that have appeared to counsel or warn humanity about impending disasters. According to believers, these visits have coincided with historic periods of rapid cultural and societal advancement. For example, in ancient Sumer (present-day Iraq) scribes wrote about white gods similar in appearance to Nordics who came to Earth to provide humanity with written languages, sciences, and architectural knowledge. Like modern ufologists, the Sumerians believed the white gods came

Did You Know?

Many ancient civilizations have left references to seeing shiny objects as well as visitors from the skies.

from the sky but then built homes under the ground where they conducted their daily business.

People in ancient Mesopotamia also described white spirits but added that they arrived on Earth in a shiny metal disk. Several millennia later, the Incas of Peru spoke of bearded, fair-skinned men from the sky, called Viracochas, who brought with them knowledge of astronomy, building skills, and the calendar. According to legend, they built the mythical city of Tiahuanacu in a single day with the aid of a magic trumpet.

A Long Way from Home

It is difficult to authenticate ancient claims of mysterious gods. However, modern beliefs are often criticized by skeptics who point out that aliens from another galaxy would have to travel for thousands of years to reach Earth. For example, the nearest star to Earth after the sun is Alpha Centauri, 24 trillion miles (38.6 trillion km) away. Even if a spacecraft could travel at 1 million miles an hour (1.6 million kph), it would take the occupants 2,500 years to reach Earth. By comparison, the *Voyager* space probe, launched by NASA in 1977, had a top speed of 40,000 miles an hour (64,374 kph) , meaning it would take 70,000 years to reach the nearest star.

Taking the physics of space travel into account, philosophy professor and renowned skeptic Robert Carroll explains why he thinks abductees commonly describe three types of alien life forms:

> There have been many reports of abduction and sexual violation by creatures who are small and bald or are white, gray, or green; have big craniums, small chins, large slanted eyes, and pointed

Grays and the U.S. Government

One popular theory about Gray aliens has them working with the U.S. government. The author Dragonbane explains on the *Above Top Secret* Web site:

> [The] relationship has resulted in many of the technological leaps of the last fifty years made by military and government science, including the F-117 stealth fighter and B-2 stealth bomber. . . . The theory goes something like this: A secret group within the government (known as the Majestic Twelve) has given the Greys several large tracts of land in the American Southwest, near the Four Corners area, on which to build

large underground bases. . . . From these locations, the Greys are able to abduct their targets with much more ease. . . .

[Many] researchers . . . believe that the government is constantly lying about its involvement in the UFO phenomenon, and is keeping much information secret, while using disinformation tactics to make all eyewitnesses appear to be foolish. The disinformation appears in various forms, from government propaganda, lies about activities, and threats to silence witnesses, to the more vocal and outspoken of "researchers" who attempt to convince others that there is no UFO phenomenon, and no such thing as extraterrestrial life. These "debunkers" use any explanation, no matter how unlikely and impossible, to explain any and all sightings.

Dragonbane, "Alien Harvest," *Above Top Secret,* 2007. www.abovetopsecret.

or no ears. How does one explain the number of such claims and their similarity? The most reasonable explanation for the accounts being so similar is that they are based on the same movies, the same stories, the same television programs, and the same comic strips. [17]

Carroll's answer does not satisfy those whose experiences with Grays, Reptoids, and Nordics have left them depressed, elated, enlightened, amazed, or paranoid. It does show, however, that creative minds can construct a number of fantastic scenarios concerning extraterrestrials. Since most abductees remember their alien captors in dreams, through hypnosis, or regressive memory therapy, it is likely some are simply recalling a dimly remembered TV show or movie. For conspiracy theorists who believe that the government is acting in consort with blood-sucking creatures from outer space, any photographic or video proof would go a long way toward dispelling doubts about such dark hypotheses. But until such time as proof can be provided, people will believe what they see, or think they saw, when discussing alien races from other planets.

CHAPTER 3

Common Threads

Alien abduction stories are often a melding of facts, fantasy, and flights of the imagination. This leaves skeptics and believers at odds, with little common ground and many points of contention. Nonetheless, both sides are inclined to agree on one point—extraterrestrial kidnapping cases seem to share a remarkable number of similarities.

The common threads that weave together abduction lore begin with the abductees themselves. Although victims can be any age, a large percentage are young adults. Their stories also tend to begin the same way. Whether they are in bed, outdoors, or in a car, they perceive an unusual aircraft accompanied by a loud humming and bright lights. Oftentimes the viewers seem physically paralyzed when the alien visitors appear and kidnap them. After being taken against their will, they seem to be transported to spacecraft through miraculous means, either by flying or being teleported through walls, ceilings, or car windows. Once aboard the spaceship, abductees often report that they are taken through a series of round rooms full of strange flashing lights, computers, or mysterious high-tech equipment. All the while, the spacecraft is abuzz with dozens of aliens moving rapidly about, performing inexplicable tasks, and generally ignoring the detainee.

Alien Couplings

Most stories culminate with the abductee being taken to a strange medical examining room where they are stripped of their clothes and subjected to surgical-like procedures. Victims report different levels of anxiety and pain as a result of these experiments, which involve peering into and probing bodily orifices or having implants inserted into their brains, organs, ears, or eyes. Men often report that they experienced rectal or colonic examinations while female abductees claim their reproductive organs were inspected to determine if they were good candidates for procreating with the aliens. Both men and women abductees have claimed to have had sexual relations with their kidnappers, as Mack explains:

> A central feature of the experience appears to be a complex sexual/reproductive "project" that, after a sequence of experiences, may result in the apparent creation of hybrid beings, toward whom the experiencers, especially young women, feel a poignantly troubled relationship. On the one hand, they feel that the creatures, which look like a cross between the aliens and humans, need their love and nurturance and that they themselves are part

"A central feature of the [abduction] experience appears to be a complex sexual/reproductive 'project.' "

—Author John Mack explaining how many abductees describe being used in reproduction experiments to create hybrid beings.

Typical Experience Described by Abductees

1. Capture
(Abductees taken from room/
area and find themselves in the "ship")

2. Examination
(a seemingly medical or physiological exam)

3. Conference
("Aliens" speak with abductees)

4. Tour
(Not always described, but some
abductees claim to be shown the ship)

5. Loss of Time
(Many abductees suffer from periods of time removed
from their memory, often coming back to them later)

6. Return
(Returned, sometimes with environmental changes)

7. Theophany
(a profound mystical experience, a feeling of
oneness with God or the universe)

8. Aftermath
(Sickness, new phobias, ridicule, etc.)

Source: Wikipedia, "Abduction Phenomenon: Profile," 2006. http://en.wikipedia.org.

of some life-creating evolutionary venture. On the other hand, they realize that they have no control over when, if ever, they can see the hybrid "baby" or "child" again, and they may resent being used as "breeders." [18]

Such was the case of a young woman named Shane Kurz who recalled under hypnosis that she had been drawn up into an oval-shaped flying saucer by a beam of light, after which she was taken to a hospital-like room aboard the craft. As is typical in such stories, Kurz says she was approached by an alien in a long white lab coat, which made her think it was a "doctor." The doctor told Kurz she was a good breeder and, like the case of Betty Hill in the early 1960s, a long needle was pushed into her navel, then removed. Another alien approached Kurz and told her telepathically that he was the leader, she was to have his baby, and she would remember nothing of the experience afterward. However, despite the allegedly advanced scientific technology available to the aliens the breeding experiment failed, and Kurz produced no alien-human hybrids.

The situation was different for an unnamed 19-year-old California woman who claimed to have given birth to a blue-skinned, web-footed baby in 1987. This occurred after she was kidnapped from a beach by blue-skinned humanoids who sexually assaulted her.

Stories of alien reproduction are not confined to females. In one of the earliest abduction stories, Boas claimed to have had relations with a beautiful, fair-haired alien woman. He also said his coupling was successful and he helped save the alien race from extinction by producing a baby with his ET beauty. Not all alien unions have happy endings, however. In the 1990s a man using the pseudonym Martin Bolton said that three young space women took over his mind and body for three years, used him for horrid experiments, and even made him pregnant. Such stories may sound bizarre to some. However, research has shown that those who claim to have had relations with extraterrestrials seem absolutely positive that they are parents of alien babies. Such was the case with Bolton.

Becoming Enlightened

Bolton was highly distressed by his experience, but oftentimes abductees feel that they have been specially chosen for the mission of reproduction. Like Boas they say they were singled out in order to save the aliens or, in other cases, help propagate the human race on another planet for a future time when Earth is destroyed. Even when reproduction is not involved, many abductees have the feeling that they were expressly selected to become enlightened or shown a path to a higher spiritual plane. Oftentimes people do not understand the lesson. As Mack writes, the "experiencers may be unclear as to just what they are to do with this knowledge but feel that it is of profound, even sacred, meaning and importance, that they are privileged to be receiving it, and that they must act in some way to bring about change."[19]

Abductees claim to be taught these mysterious lessons in several ways. Some describe vast libraries that contain normal-appearing books or computer-like plates filled with information. Others receive information through mental telepathy, intense eye-to-eye contact with giant alien lenses, or in movies shown on television-like monitors. It is also common for abductees to be transported to unearthly places where they can learn a

Many abductees describe being transported to unearthly places by aliens to learn how better to protect Earth's environment.

lesson from observing the environment around them. Photographer Carlos Diaz had such an experience while taking pictures of UFOs near Mexico City. Diaz says he was conveyed to an unfamiliar cave containing seven illuminated spheres made of yellow light. An alien invited him to enter one of the spheres which contained an alternate reality. As Diaz states, he was surrounded by images "as if I were merely an eye. I was in a forest. I could see all over. I could feel the fresh air and hear the singing birds. It was like being there. It was truly amazing. I couldn't touch anything or see my body. . . . All the things I saw in the spheres made me realize about the interaction between the smallest particle to the biggest." [20]

Like many of those who have witnessed such scenes, Diaz felt that the aliens were giving him a message about the importance of ecology. In 1996 an abductee named Nona had a similar experience that allowed her to look at nature in an entirely different way: "When they show you these environments, you can actually see the life-force in flowers and in the leaves and the water. It's like colors you've never seen before. . . . In the rain forest you could see the life existing within a leaf, within the tops of these trees. [There] were Earth spirits dancing all over the tops of those trees." [21]

In other cases the communication and learning is not very pleasant. For example, Jim Sparks claims he was abducted from Florida in 1988 and taken aboard a spacecraft where he met "small, grey, drone worker types; taller true aliens, or supervisors; and tall reptoids with big, human-shaped bodies covered with scaly, reptile skin." [22] These space creatures rigorously schooled Sparks, forcing him to learn an alien alphabet, a number system, and various inexplicable symbols. During his lessons Sparks was physically paralyzed and propped up in front of a giant television screen. The aliens first showed him the letter "A" in English and then showed him a symbol representing an alien letter "A." When he refused to cooperate and learn the lesson, the air pressure was dramatically increased until he said his head felt as if it would explode. When Sparks finally traced the alien letter A with his finger on the screen the pain stopped, and he felt a sudden feeling of euphoria. These sessions continued several days a week for years in a situation he calls "a fascinating hell, like being drafted into an alien boot camp."[23] When he was not being schooled by aliens, Sparks lived at home.

A Total Personality Change

As his lessons advanced, Sparks learned to communicate telepathically, move objects telekinetically, and to develop what he called a sixth sense, the ability to think in theoretical terms about large concepts such as Earth, its environment, and the role of human beings in the universe. Sometimes these lessons were taught at incredible speeds. Sparks claims that one time an old wrinkled alien looked into his eyes and taught him 100 things about ecology in less than one second, saying to him:

> Your air and your water are contaminated. Your forests, jungles, trees and plant life are dying. There are several breaks in your food chain. You have an amount of nuclear and biological weapons which include nuclear and biological contamination. Your planet is overpopulated. Warning: It is almost to the point of being too late unless your people act now. There are better ways of deriving your energy and food needs without causing your planet any damage. Those in power are aware of this and have the capability to put these methods into worldwide use.[24]

Like many other abductees, Sparks felt completely transformed by the experience both mentally and physically. As is typical with others who had similar abduction experiences, he felt "reprogrammed" and was able to assume a sort of duel identity with a

"It is almost to the point of being too late unless your people act now."

—An alien warning an abductee about protecting Earth's environment.

human-alien consciousness. This gave him the feeling that he was somehow interconnected with all creatures of Earth and those from other planets.

An abductee known as Sue had a similar reaction after aliens gave her environmental lessons in 1991. She saw on a giant viewing screen what the aliens called an ecological massacre, a former rain forest now bleak, barren, and devoid of any life. Before this lesson Sue had little interest in environmentalism, but afterward she became a dedicated ecologist, telling Mack of her new career: "This was not my personality. I've had a total personality change. I was never an environmentalist . . . [before] going to school" on a space ship.[25]

Visions of Doom

While abductees like Sue believe that they were taught lessons in order to help save humanity, others are shown visions so apocalyptic that they can only react with alarm, dread, panic, and despair. These abductees see tidal waves, incurable plagues, and destruction of Earth on a biblical scale. This phenomenon is so widespread that Worley was able to analyze the stories of dozens of people who said they were kidnapped by Nordic aliens:

> [The abductees] have been given warnings and scenes of a terrible cataclysmic time coming to Earth. . . . Immense fissures and volcanoes will spew forth their white hot magma over vast areas. High winds that sweep everything before them and walls of sea water miles high will be created. . . . The western USA will see only the tops of the Rocky Mountains as islands and its western re-

gions will become sea as far as western Nebraska. Los Angeles and San Francisco will be under miles of water. Same for New York and New England for that coastal region is going under. . . . In this gigantic upheaval, the St. Lawrence Bay and Great Lakes region would become a vast extension of the Atlantic Ocean reaching across the former Great Lakes and west into the Mississippi Valley and on down to the Gulf of Mexico. [26]

An abductee named Andrea was told that the volcanic explosions would begin in the Hawaiian Islands, setting off a chain reaction in volcanoes throughout the world. Eventually this will cause Earth's axis to shift, drastically changing the climate in the most populated regions of the planet.

Other abductees are told of a day of reckoning in different terms. Karin was shown a scene of a planet as it appeared from space with nuclear warheads raining down on it. After the disaster she saw cars and buildings destroyed, rubble where great cities once stood, and rivers running with toxic waste and blood. Upon viewing such scenes Karin says she became hypersensitive to Earth's pain. Whenever she sees trees cut down or roads being built she has negative physical reactions:

> I'm like a babbling brook crying. . . . Every time we tear a street it's like ugh! The Earth aches from this. I feel the soil being distressed. How do you feel soil being distressed, and how do you feel plants being distressed? And rocks? I feel like I'm dying a little bit every day. I'm dying with the

planet and with all the sorrow and the pain of all of these people that are dying around us. . . . It's enough to make you cry. [27]

Trying to Save Earth

Some abductees have a twist on the apocalypse story, saying the horrible environmental disasters actually happened to the home planet of the aliens. As proof, the abductees were shown alien news footage in which such scenes were depicted. The survivors then traveled to Earth to prevent the same thing from happening to earthlings.

Extraterrestrial environmental disasters have also been used to explain the unusual way the aliens look. For example, it is frequently said that because the aliens destroyed their planet, they were forced to build sophisticated cities underground. Living under the surface has changed the physical appearance of the creatures. Their eyes grew much larger since they were forced to live in darkness, their bodies were weakened from living with little fresh food, their faces made grotesque from existing in a damp, fetid netherworld.

Physical Problems

While apocalyptic scenes of destruction cause emotional problems for abductees, many suffer physical symptoms as well. UFO researchers say abductees have similar types of scars, lesions, bruises, and other marks. One of the most common is called a scoop mark, a small round or oval depression in the skin, about one-eighth of an inch (3.2 mm) deep, that looks as if it were scraped out of the flesh with a tiny spoon. These are believed to be the results of flesh samples taken during medical experiments. As abduction expert Budd Hopkins writes: "Over the years I have seen dozens of such strikingly similar marks and have photographed many of them."[28]

Another common mark is a straight cut from half an inch (1.3 cm) to four inches (10.2 cm) long. These are often found on the subject's arm or leg. While the purpose of these marks is unknown, they can leave nasty scars. Unusual bruises are also quite common. As with other marks, these often serve to alert the abductee that they have experienced something strange. Upon viewing the inexplicable bruise, subjects may feel compelled to undergo hypnosis or other therapy to try to remember their abduction experience.

A North Carolina woman named Mary is one such example. In April 1989 Mary woke up in the middle of the night to get a glass of water. Several hours later, with no memory of the intervening time, she found herself on the kitchen floor with the feeling that hands had been pressing down on her. She returned to bed, but in the morning she noticed a three-and-a-half-inch (8.9 cm) incision on her shoulder blade surrounded by a huge bruise. However, no blood was present on her sheets, floor, or nightgown. Several days later she showed the wound to her doctor, who remarked that it was made with surgical precision. He could not believe Mary did not recall where it came from.

Implants and Alien Inhabitations

Oftentimes scars and other wounds are the result of tiny electrical implants that have been surgically placed inside the bodies of abductees. These implants have purportedly been found under the skin and in the brains, ears, noses, teeth, legs, and glands of abductees. While a large number of abductees claim to have received such implants, the actual purpose of the implants is a matter of debate. Some say they are tracking devices used to monitor the movements of abductees, while others say they are used as communications devices. For example, Betty Stewart Dagenais of Washington State discovered an implant under the skin of her left earlobe after an abduction experience. The implant caused Dagenais much distress because she said that she could hear her abductors talking to her. More worrisome, when she thought about having the implant removed, the aliens told her she would die if she did so. Like other abductees with similar problems, there was little Dagenais could do to find relief. As Strieber writes in *Confirmation,* "She endured her [audio] encounters as best she could, the way most people endure them, in silence, alone, and without any real help."[29]

Other abductees have reported problems from their implants more disconcerting than aliens whispering in their ears. Strieber claims that the devices have also allowed aliens to take over the bodies of the abductees:

> There is a . . . suggestion that the experience involves some sort of inhabitation or . . . a kind of blurring of normal and alien selves [facilitated by the implant]. . . . Witnesses are left with a sense that the visitors are somehow inside them, or using [the implant] to look through their eyes, or [dwell] in their bodies, or [live] parallel lives to them in other worlds. In some cases there are physical sensations involved, and witnesses will report that they feel as if part of their vision is being stolen, and they somehow perceive less of the world than they did before their body began to be "shared."[30]

A Self-Perpetuating Crop

Those who have been abducted by aliens commonly say that they have been given warnings about the destruction of the environment. Jim Sparks, who claims to have been abducted hundreds of times, says that the aliens are concerned about Earth's ecology because they use it for their own mysterious purposes:

> We humans have been a self-perpetuating crop, a crop that doesn't need much tending and continues to reproduce. . . . Thank goodness they don't kill us; they just use us. . . . But now there's a problem and their investment is in trouble. They have spent a lot of time, travel and effort to farm us. But we are on an almost irreversible path of

self-destruction. Nuclear and biological weapons and their waste have polluted the air, land and water. Forests, jungles and trees are being cut down or are dying. Now there are breakdowns in the food chain and the rest of the food chain is contaminated. Overpopulation, disease and viruses beyond our grasp, with new and more complicated illnesses cropping up every day.
. . . But if we environmentally destroy ourselves, the aliens still have an excellent insurance policy. They've been collecting seeds from plants, animals and humans. Through semen and ova extraction, the aliens can start us, or other Earth life, all over again, here or somewhere else.

Quoted in Linda Moulton Howe, "Meetings with Remarkable Aliens," *Nexus Magazine*, February/March 2000. www.nexusmagazine.com.

Such implant stories remain highly controversial since no one has been able to produce a single device that scientists say is not of this planet. Oftentimes abductees claim that the devices eventually dissolved in their bodies or fell out and vanished. To explain this phenomenon they say that aliens are so advanced that they can control the implants and make them disappear at will. However, there have been cases where implants were analyzed by scientists. For example, after Dagenais died of natural causes in 1989 her family had her earlobe dissected, and the implant was extracted. In 1995 the device was given to an engineer who was not told of its origins. He conducted an analysis and discovered the implant was made of aluminum, titanium, and silicone, materials commonly used to make transmitters and receivers on Earth. Although the device purportedly had some unusual properties, the actual source of Dagenais's implant remains unknown.

Only Broadly Similar

Whether it is implants or the messages conveyed by them, ufologists point to common threads running through abduction stories to justify their belief in alien abductions. However, like many other aspects of the phenomena there is disagreement on whether or not the stories are really that similar. For example, Clancy found that after interviewing hundreds of abductees—and taking careful notes about each individual case—most abduction stories differ. According to Clancy:

> [Alien-abduction] reports are only broadly similar; in their particulars, they're very different from

one another. They vary enormously in details, such as how people get "taken" (through walls; sucked up by beams of light; ushered into UFOs), what the aliens look like (tall; short; pads on their fingers; suction cups on their fingers; webbed hands; nonwebbed hands), what they wear (nothing; orange overalls; silver track suits; black scarf and cap), what type of examination is done (needles stuck in nose; intestines pulled out . . . feet examined with manicure scissors) . . . what the purpose of the abduction is (human colonization; hybridization; education; communication; world destruction; world peace), why people get chosen ("I'm very intuitive"; "we're all abducted"; "I'm the chosen one"; "they wouldn't tell me").[31]

"[People in] Kenya or Vietnam may see weird things in the sky, but rarely anything that comes down and kidnaps them for medical or sexual purposes."

—Author Susan Clancy noting that abduction claims are uncommon outside of the U.S. and Europe.

Clancy also notes that whatever common themes exist in abduction stories, they are shared mainly by Americans, Europeans, and others from industrial societies. As she writes, people in "Kenya or Vietnam may see weird things in the sky, but rarely anything that comes down and kidnaps them for medical or sexual purposes."[32]

Nonbelievers attribute this to the fact that most Westerners are exceptionally familiar with alien life forms from reading the same books and viewing the same movies and TV shows. The popular stories find their way into the subconscious memories of millions who replay them in their dreams, adding details from their own experience. For some individuals these dreams may somehow cross over into their daily reality or are retrieved through hypnosis. This may allow them to feel fear, euphoria, stress, or a sense of purpose. They become the true believers and cannot be dissuaded from their convictions. And it is impossible to prove that abductees did not experience what they think they did. However, Clancy believes that she understands the common link in the alien abduction phenomenon:

> Aliens are entirely and extremely human, the imaginative creations of people with ordinary emotional needs and desires. We don't want to be alone. We feel helpless and vulnerable much of the time. We want to believe there's something bigger and better than us out there. And we want to believe that whatever it is cares about us, or at least is paying attention to us. That they want us. . . . That we're special. Being abducted by aliens is a culturally shaped manifestation of a universal human need.[33]

CHAPTER 4

Real or Imagined?

Since the 1960s thousands of cases of purported alien abductions have been reported. During this entire time, however, no one has produced a verifiable photo or a video as proof of an alien encounter. In fact, very few abductees, if any, even possess direct memories of their experiences aboard UFOs. As Clancy writes, they "merely *believed* they'd been abducted . . . they had no detailed personal memories of their abduction experience." For these people, their alien ordeal is only remembered by undergoing various techniques alternately referred to as regression therapy, relaxation therapy, or energy work. Whatever the name, all are basically forms of hypnosis, a technique, according to Clancy, in which a therapist "lulls the abductee into a suggestible state, in which normal reality constraints are relaxed, and then asks the abductee to vividly imagine things that might have happened."[34]

Most abductees can't recall their experience without the aid of hypnosis.

Skeptics say that subjects who are hypnotized are not remembering real events but simply reciting a "cultural script," or a narrative of an alien abduction they might have picked up in the media. Believers counter by saying that aliens do not wish to reveal their presence on Earth and have developed methods for erasing the memories of the abductees. As Jacobs writes,

Abductees are not supposed to remember what has happened to them. Forgetting is part of a systematic attempt to keep the abduction program a secret. This tactic has been extremely successful. Most abductees have no memories of any abductions even though they might have had many during their lives. The abductees whom researchers see are only a tiny minority of people who consciously remember odd events happening to them that they have been able to relate to abduction activity.[35]

Despite Jacobs's claim, however, anywhere from 10 to 25 percent remember their experience vividly without hypnosis. For example, Mack writes of an unnamed 19-year-old man in *Abduction* who clearly recalled being picked up in the middle of the afternoon by Grays. The abductee was able to describe the saucer-shaped UFO and its inhabitants with apparent total recall. "On the ship he was unable to move and was forced to lie down in a cubicle where he was bathed in laser-like light and a skin sample was taken with a cylindrical instrument."[36]

The Memory Problem

Experts evaluating the abductee situation say that even those who claim to remember their experience may be deluded. Under the best of circumstances the memory function of the brain is notoriously undependable and it becomes even more so in dangerous or traumatic situations. If a person actually was abducted by aliens and used as an unwitting guinea pig in bizarre medical experiments, chances are their memories would falter, distort reality, or repress the entire event. This would be expected even if their ability to recall was not erased by aliens. In addition, many abduction experiences are remembered years or decades after they allegedly took place. As a result, according to Jacobs:

> The [abduction] memories come out as fragmentary illogical, non-chronological pieces. Just as often, the abductee does not realize this and his or her brain automatically puts the bits and pieces of memories into a logical, chronological order. The abductee then tells a "story" of what happened to him which seems to make logical sense, and which seems as concrete as any other experience he remembers. The problem is that it is often wrong.[37]

In this situation people might say they remember things that never took place, recall details of aliens they did not see, or describe imaginary examinations or medical procedures. The problem is further complicated by the belief that aliens can manipulate the thought processes of the abductees. This would allow the space creatures to plant visions in the minds of subjects that could include scenes of paradise, apocalyptic disasters, or other hallucinations. This presents a conundrum for researchers seeking the truth, since abductees may seem absolutely convinced that they participated in an intricate chain of events that never happened.

Exploring Mysterious Episodes

While it is difficult to ascertain the truth, those who think that they have been abducted by aliens might have physical and mental problems as a result of their purported experience. Others feel that their lives have been permanently changed for unknown reasons. This causes abductees to seek help from doctors, psychiatrists, and researchers who often hear the same type of complaints. Abductees report feeling unusually weird, out of sorts, or report profound personality changes. This can be manifest in a variety of unusual behaviors. For example, in 1991 a housewife named Jerry, who dropped out of school in ninth grade and married at an early age, began writing sheaves of poems, philosophical papers, and sophisticated dissertations that were far beyond her educational level. She said, "I don't know where it's coming from,"[38] but Jerry was able to use words she did not understand and communicate ideas she felt were coming from someone else.

Others believers have physical problems such as nosebleeds, headaches, and bruises that they cannot explain. Or they experience strange events such as waking up on the kitchen floor or wandering naked in the backyard. Some suffer from personality problems, feeling depression or isolation from friends and family as never before. For whatever reason, these people attribute their problems to alien abductions. This startling realization causes them to begin their search for answers. As Mack writes:

> [Often] abductees say that there are vast areas
> of their lives that they strongly feel are outside of
> conscious recall and yet powerfully affect them on
> a day-to-day basis. Although they generally know
> that these experiences may have been traumatic
> and that their recollecting them will be disturbing,
> the majority of abductees . . . elect to investigate
> their experiences further. It is far more difficult,

they have felt, to have major episodes of their mental lives and experiences unavailable to them than it is to confront what they sense has happened, however disturbing the events may prove to be.[39]

New and Difficult Challenges

Thus far, hypnosis has been the main research tool for exploring these mysterious episodes. Researchers report that under hypnosis, many abductees are able to view their experience in a positive light or at least put it in perspective and move on with their lives. This is not to say that hypnosis is painless or a cure-all. For example, at least 25 percent of abductees say that the aliens are communicating with them, telling them they should not endeavor to recall the details of their abduction.

Whatever the circumstances, hypnosis sessions are often distressing in themselves, filled with strong emotional outbursts that express terror, rage, and wrenching grief. For this reason, the hypnotist often uses total body relaxation techniques on the subject, such as deep breathing, comforting music, and soothing imagery, to induce an artificial sleeplike state of focused concentration. The hypnotist will then ask the subject questions about the experience and steer him or her to think of safe or relaxing images if the session becomes too traumatic.

Once the session ends, subjects are asked to judge the reality of their recovered memories and decide whether they were dreams, the result of a possible mental illness, or a reaction to some disturbing event in their past, such as a near-death experience. No matter what their conclusion is, subjects frequently want to continue with the hypnosis in order to sort out their feelings and memories. However, as Jacobs warns, such sessions can have life-altering consequences:

> If you do decide to explore your memories, you can expect new and sometimes difficult challenges in your life. Any freshly recalled abduction events may prompt new, unexpected revelations. You might wonder if these disturbing events could happen again. . . . Recalling and accepting the truth of your UFO experiences can alter your relationships with the very people who are closest to you. Though some abductees find support from their family and friends, they are, unfortunately, in the minority. Talking about your UFO abduction can easily cause even family and friends to question your sanity.[40]

For this reason, abductees often join support groups to find a safe environment where they can speak freely without fear of ridicule while interacting with others who have had similar experiences.

The Hypnosis Controversy

The accuracy and efficacy of hypnotism has been called into question since physician Franz Anton Mesmer first popularized the practice in Austria in the 1770s. The most prominent controversy concerns the "hypnotic state" itself. Even in the modern world where MRIs and CAT (computerized axia tomography) scans can measure brain activity, science has not been able to prove the existence of a specific mental state called "hypnotized." People under hypnosis are simply very relaxed, in a dreamlike state comparable to when a person first drifts off to sleep at

Since most abductees remember their alien captors in dreams, through hypnosis, or regressive memory therapy, it is likely some are simply recalling a dimly remembered TV show or movie.

night. This allows them to readily respond to the suggestions of a hypnotist. As such, people under hypnosis are very suggestible and the technique may not really be what Clancy calls "psychological truth serum."[41]

Research conducted since the 1960s shows that hypnotists can purposely or accidentally plant false memories or lead a subject to vividly imagine things that never happened. One example comes from a 1983 Canadian study in which volunteers were hypnotized and told that in the past week they were awakened in the middle of the night by a noise so loud that they were frightened afterward. After the session ended, about 50 percent of the subjects were absolutely sure they had heard the sound.

In another study, volunteers were hypnotized and told to imagine that they saw a UFO, were taken aboard, and given a medical exam. While the subjects did not ultimately believe that the events took place, they did give detailed accounts of events that were remarkably similar to "real" reports given by abductees. The stories also differed little from those portrayed in popular movies such as *Close Encounters of the Third Kind.* This leads to another factor at work concerning hypnosis and alien abductions, one that might be called the Hollywood effect.

Since the 1960s dozens of popular movies have shown hypnosis to be an accurate and positive method for recovering memories. Since that time it has been widely accepted by the general public, regardless of studies to the contrary, that hypnosis is a useful tool for anyone wishing to recover lost memories. This in turn propels those who are already convinced that they have been abducted to seek out hypnotic therapy in order to remember their interactions with aliens. The experience then feeds on itself as purported abductees seek out hypnotists who believe in UFOs and extraterrestrials. In other words, believers are pre-disposed to seek out hypnotic therapy, and they are often treated by other believers. Therefore, it is not surprising that their abduction experiences are corroborated while under hypnosis. As Nick Pope, who conducted official UFO research for the British Defense Ministry, writes in *The Uninvited,* there can be a host of other problems with alien-abduction hypnosis:

> Firstly, it is entirely possible for somebody to lie while under hypnosis. Equally, it is possible for people to make mistakes about what they recollect, just as we make mistakes when trying to recall events under normal conditions. But of potentially greater significance is the fact that the subject's suggestibility makes it possible for the hypnotist to lead the witness, albeit unintentionally. This happens because the will of the hypnotic subject becomes repressed, while the hypnotist suddenly becomes a very central figure in the subject's awareness. Subjects may feel under pressure to come up with information—any information—in order not to have wasted the hypnotist's time. This information can be brought forward from anywhere in the mind. It may be genuine, but it could be drawn from dreams, fantasies, or even from books or films that the subject has encountered. There may well be no deliberate deception involved, just what is known as *confabulation,* where a subject becomes talkative in an attempt to fill any awkward silences. There can also be a

subconscious desire on the part of the subject to please the hypnotist, coming out with information that he or she feels is wanted.[42]

Significant controversy exists over the validity of hypnosis used for recall of abduction experiences.

These problems are further compounded by the growing number of researchers who have entered the alien abduction field in recent decades. These people do not need any type of

professional licenses or educational requirements to hypnotize alleged abductees. Although some researchers are psychologists or psychiatrists, many are not. Whatever their background, most use some form of hypnosis in their work. And there is no guarantee that the hypnotist is an expert at regression therapy. As Jacobs warns, people "confabulate imaginary scenarios. They remember events incorrectly. This is especially a danger when an inexperienced, incompetent, or agenda-laden hypnotist is the investigator."[43]

Occurrences of Vital Importance

As with other controversies surrounding abductions, hypnosis has its share of vociferous defenders. They point out that clinical studies of hypnosis use fabricated situations to test their theories therefore the results cannot be accurate. For example, telling someone to imagine that they were startled awake by a loud noise is not the same as interviewing someone who is repressing real memories of an actual event. As Mack explains: "[Conclusions] regarding the inaccuracy of recall . . . have been based on studies in which an environmental context was created and memory was tested in relation to events that were of [little] significance to the subject. . . . These studies, therefore, may not apply to abduction experiencers, who are highly motivated to remember accurately intense occurrences that are of the most vital importance to them."[44] In addition, after hypnotizing hundreds of abductees, Mack does not believe that most of them are motivated to make up stories in order to please the hypnotist. The ability of hypnotists to plant suggestions is also called into question, as Hopkins writes in *UFOs and Abductions:* "Several prominent UFO investigators . . . routinely employ the tactic of the 'false lead' as a test of the subject's suggestibility or desire to confabulate. In these researchers' experience, the "abductee" population forcefully resists such attempts, insisting upon the accuracy of their recall, despite the hypnotists' deliberate suggestions."[45]

For example, a false lead might be given to a subject who claimed he was about to have a medical procedure in a UFO. The hypnotist would ask him if he could see the legs that were holding up the examination table. If the subject said yes, the hypnotist would question his credibility, since no one has ever reported seeing examination tables with legs. Abductees always say the tables are on pedestals, solid blocks of stonelike material, or that the tables float in the air. As Hopkins writes, "Thus this seemingly innocuous question about seeing table legs is effective at discerning suggestibility."[46]

"The World Is a Weird Place"

The debate over regression hypnosis does not obscure the fact that thousands of people continue to believe they were kidnapped by space aliens. Those who do not believe in extraterrestrials have developed a number of theories to explain abduction phenomena.

One of the most accepted explanations has been offered by sleep researchers who have studied a condition known as sleep paralysis, a regular part of the daily sleep regimen. Normally, everyone experiences this physical loss of movement during the REM, or rapid eye movement, stage of sleep. An average person will enter four or five REM periods during a typical night, each lasting from 90 to 120 minutes, and during this time they have sequences of dreams. Sleep paralysis

Not Suffering from Mental Illness

In 1998 the Program for Extraordinary Experience Research (PEER), founded by Harvard psychologist John E. Mack, conducted standard psychological tests on 40 abductees to determine their mental states. These people were evaluated for suggestibility, personality disorders, and their ability to be easily hypnotized. Those who described the abduction experience were compared to nonabductees of comparable age, race, gender, and educational background. According to the *PEER Perspectives* newsletter:

> On the whole, the study demonstrated that those reporting alien abduction

is necessary because without it, people would move around, talk, and lash out violently while dreaming. However, about 20 percent of the population experiences sleep paralysis when they wake up in the middle of the night in a mental state somewhere in between dreaming and reality. At this juncture, experiences and those not reporting them were similar in most aspects. In addition: Those who reported encounters with alien beings are not more likely to suffer from psychological disorders than non-experiencers. Experiencers are not more vulnerable to forms of personality or perceptual manipulation (e.g. hypnotic suggestion) than non-experiencers. Those who have reported an abduction experience are not more susceptible to modes of fantasy than other non-experiencers, thus refuting the idea that reports of alien abduction are products of an over-active imagination.

"Personality Study," *Peer Perspectives*, 1997. www.johnemackinstitute.org.

they will have auditory, visual, or tactile hallucinations often accompanied by a sense of terror, shortness of breath, and a feeling of doom. A 50-year-old dermatologist named James describes his experience with sleep paralysis: "I found myself waking up in the middle of the night, seized with fear. There

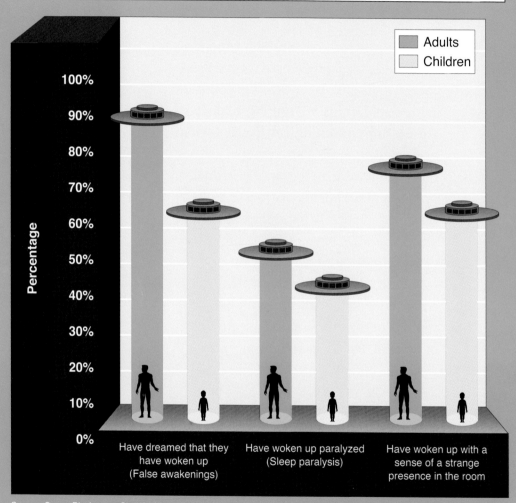

People Commonly Experience Strange Sleep Phenomena

Adults
Children

Percentage

100%
90%
80%
70%
60%
50%
40%
30%
20%
10%
0%

Have dreamed that they
have woken up
(False awakenings)

Have woken up paralyzed
(Sleep paralysis)

Have woken up with a
sense of a strange
presence in the room

Source: Susan Blackmore, *Skeptical Inquirer*, May/June 1998.

were beings standing around my bed, but I was totally para-lyzed, incapable of moving. I felt surges of electricity shooting through my body."[47]

People who wake up in such a manner require 30 to 60 seconds before their bodies can return to normal. However, if the sufferer is in a state of bewildered terror, it may seem like an eternity be-fore the hallucinations pass. When they do, the individuals may not be able to fall back asleep for many hours. This, ironically, perpetuates the condition, since sleep paralysis most often af-fects those with disrupted sleep patterns or insomnia. Anyone who suffers from this condition—and who sees creatures stand-ing around his bed night after night—may suspect that they are being abducted by aliens. As a teacher named Jon, who experi-enced problems similar to James's, commented, "Trouble sleep-ing could have a lot of causes. It could be stress. . . . It could be something worse, like being contacted by aliens. Yeah, it sounds crazy, but who knows? The world is a weird place. . . . There's a lot we don't know."[48]

It's All a Dream

An alien abduction theory similar to sleep paralysis is tied to the mental state people experience when they first fall asleep at night or first wake up in the morning. During these times people can see imagery that seems much more realistic than that which is seen in dreams. Such imagery is known as hypnagogic when experienced while falling asleep and hypnopompic when awak-ening. It is credited with providing spiritualists called shamans with dreamlike sequences in which they converse with gods, spirits, or supernatural creatures while on vision quests of wis-dom or healing. Artists, writers, and musicians also value these semiawake dream states for the inspiration they provide. For example, Paul McCartney of the Beatles said that the complete melody for the hit song "Yesterday" came to him one morning in a hypnopompic flash.

These dream states may also explain alien abductions, according to a 1996 study conducted by the *British Journal of Psychiatry.* Over 5,000 people were surveyed, and 37 percent said they experienced hypnagogic hallucinations while more than 12 percent had hypnopompic visions. The most common delusions were the sensations of falling or flying. The second most common hallucination was the feeling that someone—or something—was in the room. Like sleep paralysis, it is theoretically possible that someone who experiences hypnagogic or hypnopompic visions night after night, and does not understand what they are, might attribute their sensations to alien abductions.

Panic, Pranks, and Balls of Light

For many abductees their experience begins while lying in bed at night, giving rise to the abduction theories concerning dreams and sleep. However, those are but two theories in a long list of hypotheses as various and individual as the abductees themselves. Some say the entire abduction experience is caused by mass hysteria, the collective behavior or large numbers of people who are in a state of panic after absorbing the huge number of extraterrestrial stories in books and movies. Other scientific theories concern the electromagnetic effects of Earth, which are said to release balls of light and energy during minor earthquakes. This powerful electronic stimulus might create altered states of consciousness in some sensitive people. Finally, there are those who say that the entire alien abduction phenomenon is a mass hoax perpetrated by those craving attention, hoping to benefit finan-cially, or simply out to have some fun. This belief is backed by the fact that there have been dozens of proven abduction hoaxes over the years.

Perhaps ET kidnapping stories have been inspired by all of the above. When dealing with something as complicated as the human mind and individual experience, it is probably safe to say that the truth is out there somewhere—but might only be found at the farthest reaches of the galaxy.

CHAPTER 5

Abductions and Spiritual Convictions

Tales of alien abduction are a feature of modern life portrayed in blockbuster movies and discussed incessantly on the Internet. While the modern era of extraterrestrial kidnapping started in the late 1940s, some claim that aliens have been visiting Earth and interacting with humans for eons. Ufologists have come to this conclusion by studying ancient religious lore and imagery from India, China, Egypt, and elsewhere. For example, Indian Sanskrit texts from 13,000 B.C. tell of aliens called Vimanas or Astras that raced across the sky in antigravity machines and fought a war with people from the mythical city of Atlantis using atomic weapons on the moon. A similar tale comes from ancient China, where it was said that space aliens established a base in the Kun Lun mountains on the Tibet border and this "was the abode of immortals who flew from their secret sanctuary to the stars."[49]

One of the most famous stories ufologists connect to aliens is from the book of Ezekiel in the Bible. According to the Bible, the prophet Ezekiel reported:

> A whirlwind came out of the north, a great cloud, and a fire unfolding itself, and a brightness was about it, and out of the midst thereof was the color of amber. . . . Also out of the midst thereof

Alien Abductions are a common theme in blockbuster movies such as War of the Worlds *and* Men in Black.

came the likeness of four living creatures. And this was their appearance; they had the likeness of four living creatures . . . and every one had four faces, and every one had four wings . . . and they sparkled like the color of burnished brass.[50]

The Age-Old Narrative

Religious scholars say that the winged creatures described in Ezekiel are not space aliens but cherubim, supernatural creatures similar to angels. However, Ezekiel is but one of many stories from the Bible that ufologists say exhibit strong parallels to alien abduction tales. Skeptics say that it is not space aliens who appear in the Bible but that biblical stories are driving the alien abduction phenomenon. According to Clancy:

> The parallels between the abduction experience and the age old Christian narrative are striking. Alien abductions feature all knowing, nonhuman, advanced entities whose presence resists the explanatory power of science. The entities bring moral guidance. They tell us that time is running out, that we must change our selfish ways or our planet will be destroyed. They have come to Earth for our sake, and they are working for humanity's redemption. They want to produce superior beings. They seek not the union of God and man in Christ, but the union of aliens and humans in the hybrid. Religious creeds and UFO beliefs both require [deference] to a higher power—a power that must be accepted *on faith.* [51]

The story of Betty Andreasson Luca is a good example of how religious teachings are sometimes transformed to fit into abduction stories. Luca is a devout Christian who was purportedly abducted several times. During her first abduction, in 1967 when she was 13 years old, Luca was given the typical alien medical exam but then was taken to visit a giant bird engulfed in flames that she called "The One." The flames soon devoured the bird and left a pile of ashes from which emerged a huge worm that told Luca "I have chosen to show you the world."[52] The worm told Luca she was brought aboard the spacecraft as a test of faith. When she said she had faith in Jesus, the worm told her, "We know that you do. That is why you have been chosen. I am sending you back now. Fear not. . . . I can release you . . . through my son (Jesus)."[53] Upon hearing this, Luca said she cried tears of joy. Describing the experience later, she said there was a direct "connection between the aliens' intervention in earthly affairs and . . . Christian faith."[54]

Beliefs such as Luca's remain controversial, and religious scholars point out that God's messengers in the Bible did not use deception or disguise but identified themselves and their mission. And there are those who believe that space aliens are actually manifestations of the devil. According to the *Alien Resistance* Web site: "The alien manifestation will convince nearly everyone they have no need for a personal savior. If aliens fulfill an antichristian agenda, aren't they part of the working of error from Satan himself, setting up the Antichrist? It just seems so obvious. Aliens must therefore be agents of Satan, the fallen angels."[55]

The Unarius Academy of Science

Such debates presume that extraterrestrials indeed exist. However, when analyzing the religious aspects of UFO encounters, influential Swiss psychiatrist Carl Jung determined that the aliens were a myth invented by people to fulfill a spiritual void in their lives, or a "yearning for a savior to arrive from the sky"[56]and rescue the human race. Whatever the case, these yearnings are powerful and sometimes manifest themselves in organized groups that link alien abduction beliefs with religious imagery and teachings.

One of the earliest of such groups, the Unarius Academy of Science was founded during the burgeoning UFO craze of the 1950s. The founder of the Unarians, Ernest Norman, was a child prodigy with an unusually large head who claimed to possess psychic powers as a youth. In 1954, at the age of 50, Norman wrote the first of the Voice Series, books in which he describes a tour he took of Venus with an alien named Mal-Var. Norman claims that the Venusians are not creatures per se but energy bodies that exist in a frequency vibration, such as a radio wave, invisible to humans. However, Norman says that the most advanced humans are able to visit the Venusian capital of Azure where they study spirituality and learn to help earthlings who suffer from alcoholism, depression, and developmental disabilities.

Inspired by his discussions with the Venusians, Norman changed his name to Ioshanna and founded the Unarius academy in El Cajon, California, east of San Diego, with his wife Ruth, known as Uriel. (The name of the academy is an acronym for UNiversal ARticulate Interdimensional Understanding of Science.) During the next several decades the Normans wrote at least 20 books that taught that humanity has been regressing for hundreds of centuries. During this long period, people have forgotten their quest for self-understanding, higher consciousness, and a spiritual connection to beings in the rest of the universe.

The result of this cultural digression has been 100,000 years of poverty, disease, hatred, and war. This culminated in the invention and detonation of nuclear weapons in the 20th century.

Unarian teachings are based on Eastern religions and promote a belief in reincarnation. According to Norman, each person has lived millions of lives both on Earth and on other planets. Unarians believe that everything that occurs in an individual's life is a result of things that happened in past lives. People must become aware of their past lives and how they are interconnected in order to gain spiritual knowledge. Otherwise people will continue to suffer from tragedies caused in past lives, a concept similar to that of *karma* in Buddhism.

In this belief, Norman claimed that he was Jesus of Nazareth in a past life, with crucifixion scars to prove it. His wife claimed to have lived 55 past lives on Earth. Stretching the limits of credulity, she said that she was Buddha, Mona Lisa, Benjamin Franklin, English king Henry VIII, English queen Elizabeth I, French ruler Charlemagne, Chinese philosopher Confucius, and Russian ruler Peter the Great.

The Arrival of the Space Brothers

Ernest Norman died in 1971, but in 1984 space aliens intervened in the affairs of the Unarians once again. Ruth Norman says that at that time she traveled to the planet Vixall, where she met the planet's scientific leader, named Alta, who told her that in 2001 a spaceship from the planet Myton would land on Earth near the Bermuda Triangle in the Caribbean. During the next nine years the first ship would be followed by 31 other spacecraft. Each ship would be filled with 1,000 "Space Brothers," and by 2010, 32,000 aliens would be living on a 73-acre plot of land purchased by the

Unarians in El Cajon. Their spacecraft would be joined to one another to form buildings of a giant school. Classrooms would be filled with students learning spiritual evolution, humanity's connection to the universe, and the interconnectedness of all peoples.

Unarian literature says that the Space Brothers have the ability to begin a renaissance of peace, love, and harmony on Earth because they operate at higher mental frequencies than humans. Once their work is complete, earthlings will join the Interplanetary Confederation of the Space Brothers. Norman claims that her job would be to act as Earth's ambassador to the confederation.

During the 1980s Norman's predictions garnered quite a bit of attention, bolstered by hundreds of videos the organizations made in their state-of-the-art production studio in El Cajon. These videos, shown repeatedly on public cable-access channels, helped recruit thousands of new members to Unarius and allowed the academy to open new centers in Fort Lauderdale, Florida; Toronto and Vancouver, Canada; England; New Zealand; Nigeria; and Poland.

Ruth Norman died in 1994 and the group was taken over by Charles Spiegel. The 2001 date for the arrival of the Space Brothers came and went, causing the credibility of the academy to suffer. While Unarius claimed 500,000 members in the 1980s, by 2004 there were less than 1,000 members, and a typical meeting was drawing about 60 of the faithful. However, during her life, Ruth Norman wrote more than 80 books and produced more than 100 videos and three full-length films. Her theories about the Space Brothers continue to attract believers. And they serve as foremost examples of alleged alien-human communications that are tied to sects in the United States and throughout the world.

The Message Given by Extraterrestrials

The International Raëlian Religion, founded by Claude Vorilhon, who says he was named Raël by aliens, has a belief system similar to that of the Unarians. Raël, a former race car driver, says his life was transformed on December 13, 1973, when he was hiking in a French volcano and saw a shiny silver UFO, about 25 feet (7.6 m) in diameter, moving in total silence. A radiant being, four feet (1.2 m) tall with long black hair, almond-shaped eyes, and human in appearance, emerged from the ship and brought Raël into its craft. Once aboard, the alien purportedly told Raël that he was specifically chosen to build an alien embassy and pass along this message: "We were the ones who designed all life on earth. You mistook us for gods. We were at the origin of your main religions. Now that you are mature enough to understand this, we would like to enter official contact through an embassy."[57]

Raël soon left the spacecraft but made arrangements to meet with the alien in the same spot the next day. This time Raël found himself aboard the spacecraft taking Bible lessons. The alien began by quoting the book of Genesis: "In the beginning Elohim [God] created heaven and earth." According to *The Message Given by Extra-Terrestrials,* written by Raël about the experience, the alien explained that *Elohim* means "those who came from the sky."[58] The term was actually in reference to the race of space aliens, called the Elohim, to which Raël's ET belonged.

These creatures said they deliberately created life on Earth and then left humanity alone to progress by itself. Raël claims that the Elohim did maintain contact with the human race through prophets that include Buddha, Moses, Muhammad, and Jesus. According to Raël:

The role of the prophets was to progressively educate humanity through the Messages they taught, each adapted to the culture and level of understanding at the time. They were also to leave traces of the Elohim so that we would be able to recognize them as our Creators and fellow human beings when we had advanced enough scientifically to understand them.[59]

Since Raël was given this message along with substantial reinterpretations of the Bible to fit with his alien-creation story, Raëlism has grown to include 20,000 to 40,000 members throughout the world, with its strongest followings in France, Canada, and Japan. Convinced that the Elohim require the Raëlians to build an embassy in Israel, the group has raised over $7 million. However, the Israeli government has thus far refused Raëlian requests to build the extraterrestrial embassy in Jerusalem. And the Raëlians maintain that without an embassy, the Elohim refuse to show themselves to the rest of humanity:

Without the neutrality of an embassy, free air space and an official welcome, an unannounced and undesired landing would have enormous political, economic and social repercussions with disastrous consequences world-wide. Nor do they wish to endorse any government, religion or ideology other than that of the Raëlian Philosophy, by contacting any other institution first.[60]

Whatever the case, Raël continues to communicate his message in books, on a Web site, in a newsletter, and on an Internet radio station. Although his words have religious overtones, Raëlians do not worship the Elohim, stating: "There is no need to kneel down or to lie down with your face in the dirt . . . but rather to look up at the sky, standing proud . . . living in this day and age when we are able to understand and show love for our creators, who have given us the fantastic potential to create life."[61]

Preaching the Heaven's Gate Gospel

The word *cult* is sometimes used to describe followers of Raël or the Normans, but Raëlians and Unarians think of themselves as following a philosophy for self-improvement. They do not blindly follow orders by the leaders of their groups. However, on March 28, 1997, the term *cult* was widely used to describe Heaven's Gate after 39 of its members simultaneously committed suicide in a house in Rancho Santa Fe, California. Since the group followed teachings allegedly handed down by space aliens, the event made headlines throughout the world and brought unprecedented attention to what came to be known as a flying saucer cult.

Heaven's Gate was founded in 1975 by Marshall Applewhite, born in Texas in 1931, the son of a Presbyterian minister. Applewhite attended a theological seminary as a young man but dropped out to pursue a musical career. In 1972 Applewhite purportedly suffered a heart attack and had a near-death experience. While recuperating in a Texas hospital he met Bonnie Lu Nettles who introduced him to metaphysical studies including channeling, the practice of acting as a medium for supposed messages

Marshall Applegate, shown here, founded the sect Heaven's Gate. The sect believed that they were chosen by aliens to leave their physical bodies and ascend to "Their World."

from the spirit world. According to sociologist Robert W. Balch, who studied the Heaven's Gate sect, Applewhite and Nettles together became "absorbed in a private world of vision, dreams, and paranormal experiences that included contacts with space beings who urged them to abandon their worldly pursuits."[62]

Calling themselves The Two, Applewhite and Nettles traveled through the western United States, living at campgrounds. In 1973 Applewhite had a vision that The Two were prophets of the Book of Revelation and that they had 1,260 days to spread what he called "a message of truth." After that time, enemies would kill The Two and they would ascend to heaven in a spaceship. According to Jeffrey K. Hadden and John A. Saliba on the Religious Movements Web site, "With a belief system that combined elements of Christian scripture . . . and other assorted metaphysical teachings, along with a healthy dose of contemporary folk wisdom about UFOs, the two space-age shepherds set out to preach their gospel."[63] While serious about their message, Applewhite and Nettles first changed their names, respectively, to Guinea and Pig, later settling on Bo and Peep.

Entering the Kingdom Level Above Human

During a Los Angeles lecture, Bo and Peep convinced about 25 men and women to follow them to Oregon in order to start a UFO religion. By 1975 the as yet unnamed sect had grown to several hundred followers. The following year Bo claimed that he and Peep were actually space aliens who had moved into the bodies of Applewhite and Nettles. They explained this transformation on the *Heaven's Gate* Web site: "In the early 1970's, two individuals . . . incarnated into (moved into and took over) two human bodies that were in their forties. I moved into a male body, and my partner . . . took a female body. (We called these bodies "vehicles," for they simply served as physical vehicular tools for us to wear while on a task among humans)."[64]

The followers of Bo and Peep came to believe that they were taking orders from space aliens who revealed their wisdom during intense programming sessions. Hadden and Saliba explain the message:

> According to the teachings of The Two, some two thousand years ago extraterrestrials from the Kingdom of Heaven passed this way to survey their garden Earth and concluded that perhaps it had evolved to a point where it would be useful to send down one being from the "level above."

Earthlings, it turned out, were not ready to enter the "Kingdom Level Above Human." The one they sent was killed and [devilish] influences continued to dominate the Earth. Bo and Peep came to believe that they were extraterrestrials who offered humans yet another chance to move to a higher evolutionary level. Here, the Christian message of sin and salvation was intermingled with elements of Eastern religious traditions in which seekers attempt to break out of a cycle of death and reincarnation. The Heavenly Kingdom that Bo and Peep came to tell of was not simply spiritual, but literal. The method of transportation to this Kingdom was a spacecraft. The price one paid for a "boarding pass" to this higher level was a disciplined life which would bring about a bodily metamorphosis they likened to the transformation from a caterpillar to a beautiful butterfly. Called "Human Individual Metamorphosis" (HIM), this process would literally transform human physiology.[65]

In order to make this transformation, members of the group followed strict rules, including abstinence from sex, drugs, and alcohol. They cut off contact with friends, relatives, and the outside world, shaved their heads, sold their worldly possessions, and changed their names. (The Two again changed their names, Bo to Do and Peep to Ti.) Some of the males, in order to remain celibate, castrated themselves. The Two took total control over members' lives, using a vocabulary loaded with ufology and alien symbolism.

The Heaven's Gate members believed that the method of transportation to the "Heavenly Kingdom" was an alien spacecraft.

Hitching a Ride on a Comet

In 1996 the followers of The Two settled in a luxury estate in the wealthy San Diego suburb of Rancho Santa Fe, paid for by the group's thriving Internet design company called Higher Source.

The Ancient Astronaut Theory

Some ufologists state that humanity was created by ancient astronauts, or space aliens, many eons ago. They support this hypothesis by using unconventional translations of clay tablets written by the ancient Sumerians. Author Alan F. Alford explains the ancient astronaut theory:

> Ancient astronaut writers believe that a race of intelligent extraterrestrial beings visited and/or colonized Earth in the remote past, whereupon they upgraded the primitive hominid *Homo erectus* by means of genetic engineering to create the human race as we know it. . . .

Although they had been calling themselves The Group, they now assumed the name Heaven's Gate. Around the same time, astronomers Alan Hale and Thomas Bopp announced the discovery of a comet that would pass very close to the sun on April 1, 1997.

> Evidence for this idea is found . . . in the myths of ancient civilizations which describe human-like gods coming down from the heavens and creating mankind 'in their own image.' . . . According to [this] interpretation of the ancient myths, an extraterrestrial race of gods known as 'the Anunnaki' came down to the Earth 445,000 years ago from a planet known as Marduk or Nibiru—a planet which remains in our solar system on a vast elliptical orbit of 3,600 years. These Anunnaki-gods then created *Homo sapiens,* partly in their own image, using a process of genetic engineering, with the aim of using this hybrid species as a slave race.

Alan F. Alford, "Ancient Astronaut Hypothesis," Official Web Site of Alan F. Alford, 2004. www.eridu.co.uk.

Comet Hale-Bopp was expected to be one of the brightest seen in more than a century.

In the UFO community rumors began to circulate that Comet Hale-Bopp was followed by an alien spaceship. On the *Heaven's*

Gate Web site, this news was celebrated with the announcement "Hale-Bopp Brings Closure to Heaven's Gate":

> Hale-Bopp's approach is the "marker" we've been waiting for—the time for the arrival of the spacecraft from the Level Above Human to take us home to "Their World"—in the literal Heavens. Our 22 years of classroom here on planet Earth is finally coming to conclusion— "graduation" from the Human Evolutionary Level. We are happily prepared to leave "this world" and go with Ti's crew.[66]

While this announcement meant little to outsiders who might have happened upon it, inside the Rancho Santa Fe home cult members commenced preparation to abandon their physical bodies, called "containers," so that their souls could ascend to heaven. On March 28, 1997, 39 members of Heaven's Gate ate pudding and applesauce laced with massive doses of barbiturates and washed it down with vodka. The lethal mixture killed them within 30 minutes. In a written statement obtained by the media, Do wrote: "By the time you read this we'll be gone—several dozen of us. We came from the Level of Above Human in distant space and we have now exited the bodies that we were wearing for our earthly task, to return to the world from whence we came—task completed."[67]

"Part of the Future"

There is ample evidence that Heaven's Gate members were not coerced but willingly killed themselves so that alien gods would save them from the travails of their earthly existence. While such blind faith is rare, there are countless believers who state that humankind was created by extraterrestrials or that space aliens are guiding earthlings through surrogates like Do. While the Heaven's Gate group has been universally condemned, many who subscribe to such visions do not see their beliefs as negative but as a way to achieve eternal life. As Ruth Norman writes in *Preparation for the Landing,*

> [We] have been given the opportunity to help in the progressive evolution of Earth, and it is my humble opinion that we . . . will gain greatly by this. Not for self, but we will gain a greater awareness of the Father, and you, as a result, will become part of the future. And in this pioneering effort, we will bring about the movement of planet Earth into its proper orbit.[68]

NOTES

Introduction: Visitors from Space

1. Quoted in Evelyn Galson, "Francis Abduction On-going in New Jersey, 2004," *Casebook.* February 2005. www.ufocasebook.com.
2. Quoted in Ellie Crystal, "Alien Abductions," CrystalLinks, 2007. www.crystalinks.com.
3. Quoted in Crystal, "Alien Abductions."

Chapter 1: Kidnapped by Aliens

4. Quoted in Terry Melanson, "Antonio Villas Boas: Abduction Episode Ground Zero," Illuminati Conspiracy Archive, May 10, 2005. www.conspiracyarchive.com.
5. Quoted in B.J. Booth, "Betty and Barney Hill Abduction, Part 1," *UFO Casebook,* 2006, www.ufocasebook.com.
6. Susan A. Clancy, *Abducted.* Cambridge, MA: Harvard University Press, 200. p. 101.
7. John E. Mack, *Abduction.* New York: Charles Scribners' Sons, 1994, p. 38.
8. David M. Jacobs, "Some Thoughts About the Twenty-First Century," International Center for Abduction Research, 2006, www.ufoabduction.com.

Chapter 2: Alien Life Forms

9. Quoted in UFO Evidence, "About Mothmen and Men in Black," 2007. www.ufoevidence.org.
10. Dragonbane, "Alien Harvest," Above Top Secret, 2007. www.abovetopsecret.com.
11. Quoted in Aileen Garoutte, "UFO Experiences," Blog Spot, October 16, 2006. http://ufoexperiences.blogspot.com.
12. Quoted in Garoutte, "UFO Experiences."

13. Karinya, "The Reptoids, Otherwise Known as the Lizards from Orion," 2006. www.karinya.com.
14. Donald Worley, "Nordic Alien Type Experiences," Alien Abduction Experience and Research, 2006. www.abduct.com.
15. Quoted in Worley, "Nordic Alien Type Experiences."
16. Worley, "Nordic Alien Type Experiences."
17. Robert Carroll, "Alien Abductions," *Skeptics Dictionary,* 2005. http://skepdic.com.

Chapter 3: Common Threads

18. John E. Mack, *Passport to the Cosmos.* New York: Crown, 1999, pp. 13-14.
19. Mack, *Passport to the Cosmos,* pp. 15-16.
20. Quoted in Mack, *Passport to the Cosmos,* p. 101.
21. Quoted in Mack, *Passport to the Cosmos,* p. 87.
22. Quoted in Linda Moulton Howe, "Meetings with Remarkable Aliens," *Nexus Magazine,* February/March 2000. www.nexusmagazine.com.
23. Jim Sparks, "From the Edge of Experience," Peer Perspectives, 1997. www.peermack.org.
24. Quoted in Howe, "Meetings with Remarkable Aliens."
25. Quoted in Mack, *Passport to the Cosmos,* p. 90.
26. Donald Worley, "The Cataclysmic Future of the Midwest," Alien Abduction Experience and Research, 2006. www.abduct.com.
27. Quoted in Mack, *Passport to the Cosmos,* p. 99.
28. Quoted in David M. Jacobs, ed., *UFOs and Ab-*

ductions. Lawrence: University Press of Kansas, 2000, p. 225.

29. Whitley Strieber, *Confirmation.* New York: St. Martin's, 1998, p. 178.
30. Strieber, *Confirmation,* pp. 171-72.
31. Clancy, *Abducted,* pp. 82-83.
32. Clancy, *Abducted,* p. 103.
33. Clancy, *Abducted,* p. 104.

Chapter 4: Real or Imagined?

34. Clancy, *Abducted,* p. 32.
35. David M. Jacobs, "Examining Memory," International Center for Abduction Research, 2006. www.ufoabduction.com.
36. Mack, *Abduction,* p. 21.
37. Jacobs, "Examining Memory."
38. Quoted in Mack, *Abduction,* p. 112.
39. Mack, *Abduction,* p. 21.
40. David M. Jacobs, "Pros and Cons of Investigating Unusual Personal Experiences," International Center for Abduction Research, 2006. www.ufoabduction.com.
41. Clancy, *Abduction,* p. 59.
42. Nick Pope, *The Uninvited.* Woodstock, NY: Overlook, 1997, pp. 51-52.
43. Jacobs, "Pros and Cons."
44. Mack, *Abduction,* p. 24.
45. Quoted in Jacobs, *UFOs and Abductions,* p. 220.
46. Quoted in Jacobs, *UFOs and Abductions,* p. 220.
47. Quoted in Clancy, *Abduction,* p. 34.
48. Quoted in Clancy, *Abduction,* pp. 40-41.

Chapter 5: Abductions and Spiritual Convictions

49. Quoted in "A Brief UFO History," UFOs at Close Site, February 9, 2005. www.ufologie.net.
50. Quoted in Keith Thompson, *Angels and Aliens.* New York: Fawcett Columbine, 1993, p. 71.
51. Clancy, *Abducted,* pp. 151-52.
52. Quoted in Brenda Denzler, *The Lure of the Edge.* Berkeley and Los Angeles: University of California Press, 2001, p. 126.
53. Quoted in Denzler, *The Lure of the Edge,* p. 126.
54. Quoted in Denzler, *The Lure of the Edge,* p. 125.
55. Alien Resistance, "Stop Alien Abductions," 2006. www.alienresistance.org.
56. Quoted in Jacobs, *UFOs and Abductions,* p. 145.
57. Quoted in Raëlian Movement, "Message of the Designers," 2005. www.rael.org.
58. Raël, *The Message Given by Extra-Terrestrials.* Geneva, Switzerland: Raëlian Religion, 1998, p. 20.
59. Raëlian Movement, "Message of the Designers."
60. Raëlian Movement, "FAQ—Why Do They Need an Embassy?" 2005. www.rael.org.
61. Quoted in Faye Whittemore, "Raëlians," Religious Movements, March 11, 2001. http://religiousmovements.lib.virginia.edu.
62. Quoted in Jeffrey K. Hadden and John A. Saliba, "Heaven's Gate," Religious Movements, March 25, 2005. http://religiousmovements.lib.virginia.edu.
63. Hadden and Saliba, "Heaven's Gate."
64. Bo, "'95 Statement by an E.T. Presently Incarnate," Heaven's Gate, January 1997. www.heavensgate.com.
65. Hadden and Saliba, "Heaven's Gate."
66. Heaven's Gate, "Heaven's Gate—How and When It May Be Entered," January 1997. www.heavensgate.com.
67. Quoted in Todd S. Purdum, "Tapes Left by Cult Suggest Comet Was the Sign to Die," *New York Times,* March 28, 1997. www.nytimes.com.
68. Ruth Norman, *Preparation for the Landing.* El Cajon, CA: Unarius Educational Foundation, 1987, p. 490.

WORKS CONSULTED

Books

Preston Dennett, *Extraterrestrial Visitations: True Accounts of Contact.* St. Paul: Llewellyn Publications, 2001. Ten original accounts of very close contact with UFOs and aliens, as told by witnesses in their own words. Most of cases come from fully conscious experiences, as opposed to cases retrieved through hypnosis. Several of the stories present new information that is highly controversial and not commonly reported in UFO literature.

Alva Press, *The World's Greatest UFO and Alien Encounters.* Edison, NJ: Alva, 2003. A comprehensive compilation of extraterrestrial activity previously published in books, magazines, and newspapers.

Eric Elfman, *Almanac of Alien Encounters.* New York: Random House, 2001. A wealth of UFO sighting reports from ancient Egypt and China to the present with samples from the United States, Israel, Switzerland, New Guinea, France, and Cuba.

Bill Fawcett (ed), *Making Contact: A Serious Handbook for Locating and Communicating With Extraterrestrials.* New York: Morrow, 1997. A manual for interacting with space aliens that includes case studies, diagrams, guidelines for interplanetary contact, and opinions and advice from leading scientist, UFO researchers, and extraterrestrial life exerts. This book examines many possible levels of contact and details the potential hazards involved in human-ET meetings.

Judith Herbst, *Aliens.* Minneapolis: Lerner, 2005. An investigation into several well-known alien abduction accounts as well as theories aimed at explaining the truth of these claims.

Budd Hopkins, *Witnessed: The True Story of the Brooklyn Bridge UFO Abductions.* New York: Pocket Books, 1996. The bestselling, allegedly true story of a motorcade carrying international diplomats, including a UN representative, who were kidnapped by three ugly gray aliens in a reddish-orange UFO in the middle of New York City.

Lisette Larkins, *Calling on ET's: 11 Steps to Inviting Your Own UFO Encounters.* Charlottesville, VA: Hampton Roads, 2003. The author, an alien abductee, offers readers 11 simple steps they can use to invite their own otherworldly contact.

Terry Matheson, *Alien Abductions: Creating A Modern Phenomenon.* Amherst, NY: Prometheus Books, 1998. An exploration of alien abduction throughout history. The author explains that traditional aliens were friendly or merely curious—quite different from today's ugly, fierce, sinister creatures from recent abduction narratives.

Tamara L. Roleff, ed., *Alien Abductions.* San Diego: Greenhaven, 2003. Ufologists, abductees, and skeptics examine whether humans have really been abducted by extraterrestrials.

For Further Research

Books

Eric Elfman, *Almanac of Alien Encounters*. New York: Random House, 2001. A wealth of UFO sighting reports from ancient Egypt and China to the present with samples from the United States, Israel, Switzerland, New Guinea, France, and Cuba.

Judith Herbst, *Aliens*. Minneapolis: Lerner Publications, 2005. An investigation into several well-known alien abduction accounts as well as theories aimed at explaining the truth of these claims.

Lisette Larkins, *Calling on Extraterrestrials: 11 Steps to Inviting Your Own UFO Encounters*. Charlottesville, VA: Hampton Roads Publications, 2003. The author, an alien abductee, offers readers 11 simple steps they can use to invite their own otherworldly contact.

Tamara L. Roleff (ed), *Alien Abductions*. San Diego: Greenhaven Press, 2003. Ufologists, abductees, and skeptics examine whether humans have really been abducted by extraterrestrials.

Gloria Skurzynski, *Are We Alone? Scientists Search for Life in Space*. Washington, DC: National Geographic Society, 2004. A clearheaded look at the theories behind flying saucers, extraterrestrial civilizations, and scientific proof of life on other planets.

Web Sites

Alien Abduction Experience and Research (www.abduct.com). A site maintained by abduction researcher Donald Worley with alien abduction incidents, abduction blogs, predictions of disasters, photos, and other information concerning kidnappings by space creatures.

The A–Z of Alien Species (www.ufos-aliens.co.uk/cosmicspecies.htm). This site covers the details of various aliens, including Grays, Reptilians, and Nordics, as described by abductees.

Heaven's Gate, (www.heavensgate.com). The web site of the UFO cult preserved exactly as it appeared in 1997 when 39 members committed suicide so their souls could purportedly board spaceship they believed was passing close to earth.

The International Center for Abduction Research (www.ufoabduction.com). The International Center for Abduction Research (ICAR) is an organization devoted to the dissemination of trustworthy information about UFO abductions and to providing accurate information to therapists and other individuals who are interested in abductions.

Message from the Designers (www.rael.org). A Web site maintained by the Raëlian Movement, a group that believes space aliens created all life on Earth and uses recognized religious prophets to convey their message to humanity.

Mutual UFO Network (www.mufon.com). Founded in 1969, the Mutual UFO Network, or MUFON, is one of the oldest and most respected organizations that researches and investigates UFO phenomena.

Religious Movements Home Page Project, University of Virginia (http://religiousmovements.lib.virginia.edu). A web site with detailed profiles of more than 200 religious groups with articles on Heaven's Gate, the Raëlians, and other UFO sects.

INDEX

I

Incas, 37
India, 78
industrialized societies, 57–58
International Center for Abduction
    Research, 23
International Raëlian Religion,
    85–87
Interrupted Journey, The (Fuller), 18
Ioshanna, 82–83
Israel, 86

J

Jacobs, David M.
    on confabulation during hypnosis,
        70
    on erasure of memories, 60–61
    on faulty memories, 62
    on recovering memories, 65
    on teaching by ETs, 23
James (abductee), 73, 75
Jenny (abductee), 22–23
Jerry (abductee), 63
Jung, Carl, 82

K

Karin (abductee), 50–51
Karinya Spiritual Awareness (Web
        site), 32
Kennedy, John F., assassination of, 27
Keyhoe, Donald, 17
Kun Lun mountains, 78
Kurz, Shane, 44

L

Luca, Betty Andreasson, 81
Lutrell, John H., 18

M

Mack, John Edward
    on accuracy of research about
            hypnosis, 70
    on invasive procedures, 22
    program founded by, 72–73
    on reproduction experiments, 42,
            44
    on victims
        ability to remember without
                hypnosis, 61
        feelings of enlightenment, 45
        ordinariness of, 6–7
        search for answers, 63–64
Mal-Nor (ET), 82
Marduk (planet), 93
Mars, 9
Mary (abductee), 52
mass hoax, 76–77
mass hysteria, 76
Matheson, Terry, 7
McCartney, Paul, 76
media. *See* popular culture
medical examinations
    painful, 9, 20–22
    pregnancy tests, 14
    scars from, 51–52
    similarities among, 42, 57
    surgical implants, 35, 52–53, 56
Meehan (abductee), 34–35
memory
    erased, 60–61
    planting, 67
    problems, 61–62
    recovering, 64, 65
Mesmer, Franz Anton, 65
Mesopotamia, 37
*Message Given by Extra-Terrestrials,
        The* (Raël), 85
Miami, Florida, 35
mind-control technique, 30–31
missing persons, 32
Monotrons, 35
mothman, 24
movies. *See* popular culture
Myton (planet), 83

N

Nazis, 26–27
Nettles, Bonnie Lu, 87–90
Nevada, 27, 28 (map)7
New York Times (newspaper), 24
Nibiru (planet), 93
nightmares, 14, 15, 18
Nona (abductee), 47
Nordics, 34–37
Norman, Ernest, 82–83
Norman, Ruth, 82–84, 95
novels, 19–20

O

Outer Limits (television program),
        17–18

P

Paul (abductee), 22
Peep, 89, 90
PEER Perspectives (newsletter), 72–73
Peter (Nordic), 35
physics of space travel, 37
Pig, 89
Play-Station2 *Destroy All Humans!*
        (video game), 26
Pleiadeans. *See* Nordics
Pleiades (star system), 34
Pope, Nick, 68–69
popular culture
    fascination with spacecraft and ETs,
            17–18
    Grays in, 26
    Hollywood effect, 67
    hypnosis and, 67–68
    increase in abductions after
            programs on media, 17–19
    is shared by industrialized societies,
            57–58
    novels, 19–20
    provides information for reports, 60
predictions. *See* warnings
Preparation for the Landing (Ruth
        Norman), 95

Program for Extraordinary
Experience Research
(PEER), 72–73
public opinion
about victims, 7
knowledge of spaceships, 9, 10

R

radiation poisoning, 12
Raël, 85–87
rape, 29–30
regression therapy. *See* hypnosis
regressive hypnosis. *See* hypnosis
reincarnation, 83
relaxation therapy. *See* hypnosis
religion
Bible
ETs in, 79–80
Heaven's Gate and, 88
as source of predictions, 36
Eastern influence, 83
ETs as messengers of God or
Satan, 81
ETs as saviors, 82
International Raëlian Religion,
85–87
mystical experience, 43
Unarians, 82–84
Religious Movements (Web site),
88–90
reproduction experiments
to form alien-human hybrids,
11, 27
of Grays, 16
similarities among, 42, 44
Reptilian-Gray crossbreeds, 33–34
Reptilians. *See* Reptoids
Reptoids
control Grays, 29
control victims, 30–31
description, 29
nobility, 31–33
research, 70–71
see also hypnosis
Reticulans. *See* Grays
Roswell, New Mexico, 26

S

Saliba, John A., 88–90
Sanskrit texts, 78
Sarah (abductee), 36
Satan, 81
scoop marks, 51
September 11, 2001 terrorist attack, 27
Seven Sisters (star system), 34
shamans, 75
Simon, Benjamin, 16, 17, 18
sixth sense, 48
sleep paralysis, 71–73, 74 (graph), 75
sleep phenomena
hypnagogic imagery, 75–76
percentage of people having, 74
(graph)
sleep paralysis, 71–73, 75
South Park (television program), 26
Space Brothers, 83–84
spaceships
confirmed by radar, 14
descriptions, 5, 10, 13, 41–42, 43
pre-World War II sightings, 8–9
public knowledge of, 9, 10
space travel physics, 37
Sparks, Jim, 47–49, 54–55
Spiegel, Charles, 84
Stargate (television program), 26
star maps, 15, 16, 18
straight cuts, 52
Streiber, Whitley, 19–20, 53
Sue (abductee), 49
Sumerians, 36–37, 92–93

T

telekinetic powers, 34–35, 48
telepathic communication, 6, 32, 34,
48
Telosians. *See* Nordics
Telosia (planet), 34
theophany, 43
Thompson, Simon Estes, 9–10
Ti, 90
Tiahuanacu (mythical city), 37

time warps, 11, 13, 43
Two, The, 88–90

U

"UFO Chiller: Did THEY Seize
Couple?" (Lutrell), 18
UFO Incident, The (TV movie),
17–18
UFOs. *See* spaceships
Unarius Academy of Science, 82–84
Uninvited, The (Pope), 68–69
United Press International (UPI, news
service), 18
Universal Articulate Interdimensional
Understanding of Science.
See Unarius Academy of
Science
Uriel, 82–84
U.S. government and Grays, 26, 27,
38–39

V

Venus, 10, 82
vermin, 31
victims
characteristics of
ordinariness of, 6–7
similarities among, 41–42
suggestibility and, 72–73
usually area from industrialized
societies, 57–58
controlled by Reptoids, 30–31
media and, 18
need to feel special, 59
number of, 6, 19
public treatment of, 7
reprogramming of, 48–49, 50–51
as specially chosen, 85
typical experience, 43
see also aftermath of abductions
video games, 26
Vimanas, 78
Viracochas, 37
Vixall (planet), 83
Voice Series books, 82
Vorilhon, Claude, 85

About the Author

Stuart A. Kallen is a prolific author who has written more than 200 nonfiction books for children and young adults over the past 20 years. His books have covered countless aspects of human history, culture, and science from the building of the pyramids to the music of the 21st century. Some of his recent titles include *History of World Music, Romantic Art,* and *Women of the Civil Rights Movement.* Kallen is also an accomplished singer-songwriter and guitarist in San Diego, California.